D0690618

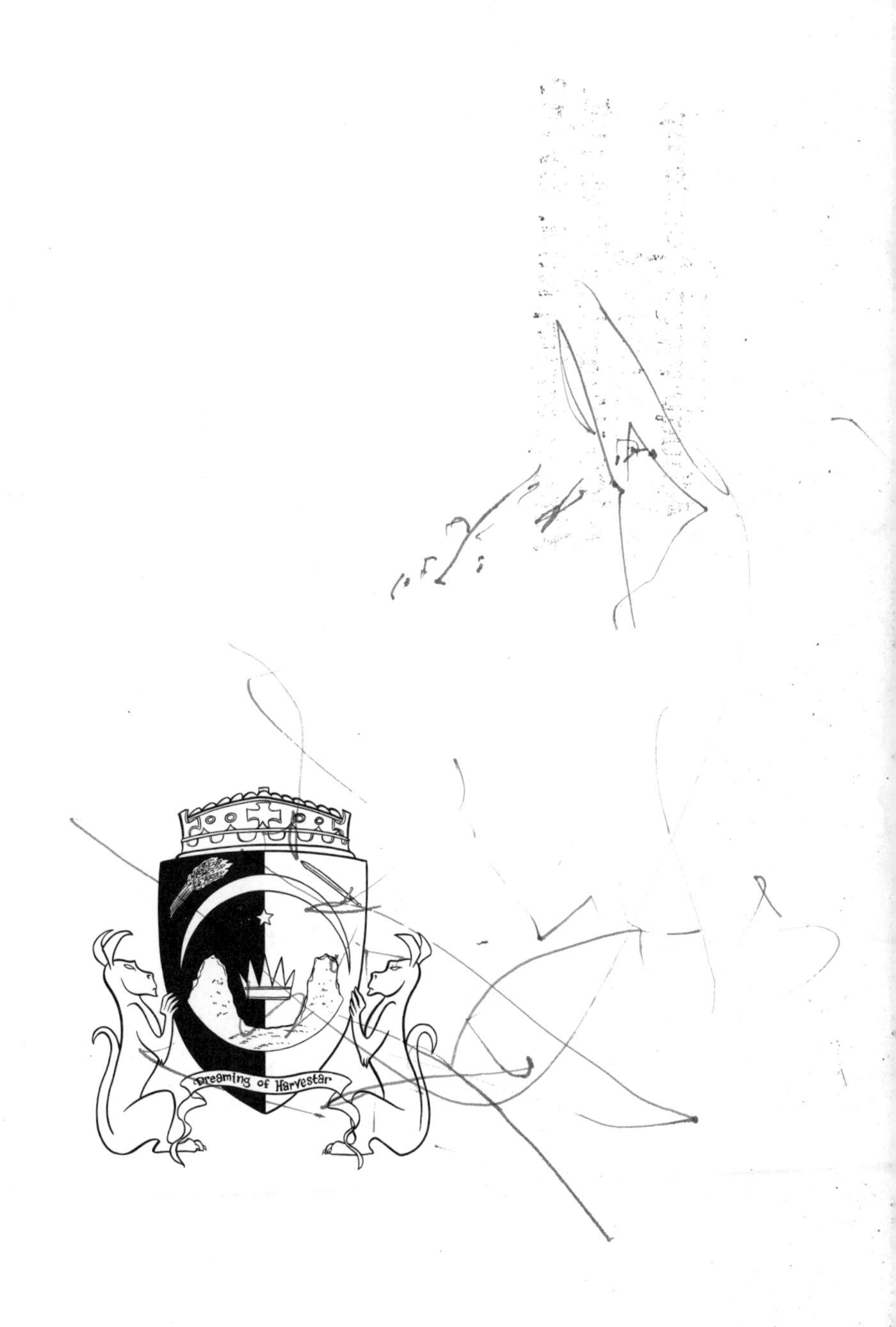
Dreaming of Harvestar

OTHER BOOKS BY JEFF SMITH

THE FIRST TRILOGY

BONE VOLUME ONE: OUT FROM BONEVILLE

BONE VOLUME TWO: THE GREAT COW RACE

BONE VOLUME THREE: EYES OF THE STORM

BONE READER: THE MAKING OF THE FIRST TRILOGY

(COMING SPRING, 1997)
BONE VOLUME FOUR: THE DRAGONSLAYER

Eyes Of The Storm

Volume Three: Eyes Of The Storm

Jeff Smith

Cartoon Books
Columbus, Ohio

THIS BOOK IS FOR
MY PARENTS
BARBARA GOODSELL
AND
WILLIAM EARL
SMITH

 Acknowledgements: The Harvestar Family Crest designed by Charles Vess, and color airbrush on dustjacket by David Reed.

For information write:
Cartoon Books
P.O. Box 16973
Columbus, OH 43216

Hardcover ISBN: 0-9636609-7-7
Softcover ISBN: 0-9636609-6-9

Library of Congress Catalog Card Number: 95-68403

10 9 8 7 6 5 4 3 2

Printed in Canada

AFTER BEING RUN OUT OF BONEVILLE, THE THREE BONE COUSINS, FONE BONE, PHONEY BONE, AND SMILEY BONE, ARE SEPARATED AND LOST IN A VAST UNCHARTED DESERT.
ONE BY ONE, THEY FIND THEIR WAY INTO A DEEP, FORESTED VALLEY FILLED WITH WONDERFUL AND TERRIFYING CREATURES...

BONE™
HIGH ALOFT IN TH' CROSS-TREES WAS THAT MAD TASHTEGO!
AS HE STOOD HOVERING OVER YOU HALF SUSPENDED IN AIR, SO WILDLY AND EAGERLY PEERING TOWARDS THE HORIZON, YOU WOULD HAVE THOUGHT HIM SOME PROPHET OR SEER BEHOLDING THE SHADOWS OF FATE, AND BY THOSE WILD CRIES ANNOUNCING THEIR COMING---
THAR SHE BLOWS! THERE! THERE! THERE!! SHE BLOWS! SHE BLOWS!
WHAT IN TH' WORLD IS GOIN' ON HERE?!
OH, HELLO, MIZ POSSUM! I WAS JUST READING FROM MOBY DICK!
OH, MY! IS THAT WHAT YOU WERE DOIN'?! READ SOME MORE SO I CAN HEAR IT, TOO!
UH...
YOU WANT TO HEAR ABOUT MOBY DICK?! ARE YOU SURE?!
WHY NOT? YOU WERE READING IT TO THORN!
I'VE BUILT UP A TOLERANCE.

MAYBE I'LL READ IT LATER. SO, WHAT BRINGS YOU BY, MIZ POSSUM?
OH, YOU KNOW **ME**, BONE! I'M ALWAYS **CHECKIN' UP** ON THINGS -- MAKIN' SURE EVERYBODY'S **OKAY**!

I SEE YOU BEEN WORKIN' ON TH' **FARMHOUSE**! HOW'S THAT GOIN'?

WE'RE MAKING **PROGRESS**. THE **RAT CREATURES** DID A LOT OF **DAMAGE**!
OH, I **KNOW**! ISN'T IT **TERRIBLE**? AT LEAST YOU PATCHED THAT **HOLE** IN TH' WALL!

AN' NOT A **MOMENT** TOO SOON! YOU NEVER KNOW WHEN THOSE **HOOLIGANS** MIGHT COME BACK!

GRAN'MA THINKS TH' RAT CREATURES WILL STAY AWAY FOR A WHILE.
WELL, YOU'RE PROBABLY ALL RIGHT DURIN' TH' **DAYTIME**, BUT DON'T TAKE CHANCES AT **NIGHT**! YOU'RE NOT STILL SLEEPIN' **OUTSIDE**, ARE YOU?

NO, M'AM! WE'RE ALL SLEEPIN' INDOORS! IN TH' **BIG ROOM** DOWNSTAIRS!
AS SOON AS LUCIUS AND SMILEY FINISH THE **ROOF**, WE'LL MOVE INTO THE BEDROOMS **UPSTAIRS**.
THAT'S GOOD, ANYWAY...

AN' WHAT ABOUT THAT GREEDY COUSIN OF YOURS? PHONEY BONE? I HEAR HE CAUSED QUITE A RUCKUS AT THAT COW RACE!
GRAN'MA'S MAKIN' HIM SHOVEL OUT TH' BARN. . .
WITH A SPOON!

SERVES HIM RIGHT! WELL, I'D LOVE TO STAY AN' GOSSIP ALL DAY, BUT I LEFT TH' KIDS WITH MIZ HEDGEHOG, AN' I PROMISED I WOULDN'T BE GONE LONG.
HERE, BONE! I BROUGHT THIS FOR YOU!

SILLY ME! I ALMOST FORGOT TO ASK . . . TH' BOYS WANTED ME TO FIND OUT HOW YOUR GRANDMOTHER DID IN TH' RACE, DEAR!
SHE WON!

THAT'S WONDERFUL! OKAY! NOW I REALLY MUST BE LEAVING! IF YOU NEED ANYTHING AT ALL, YOU JUST HOLLER, YOU HEAR?

OH! AND THAT STUFF IN TH' PAN? IF YOU HAVE ANY LEAKS IN THAT NEW ROOF OF YOURS - - - -

- - JUST SMEAR THAT GOO OVER IT! SEALS UP ANYTHING! GUARANTEED!
THANKS FOR DROPPING BY, MIZ POSSUM.

SHE'S RIGHT ABOUT NOT TAKING CHANCES AFTER DARK. WE SHOULD START BACK.
OKAY.

WHO'S TURN IS IT TO STAY UP ON WATCH DUTY?
MINE.

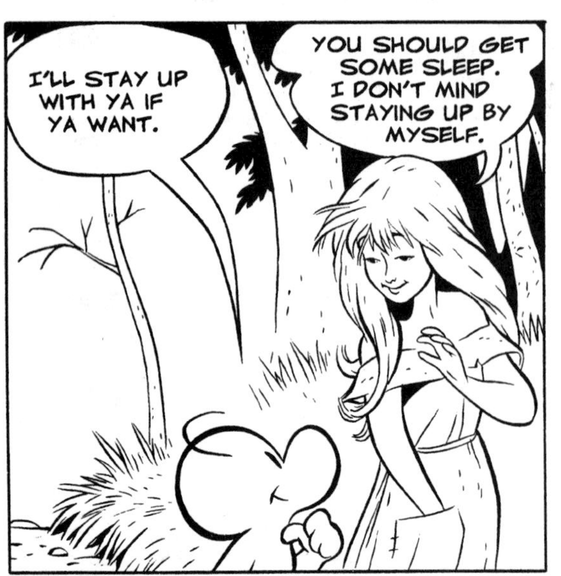
I'LL STAY UP WITH YA IF YA WANT.
YOU SHOULD GET SOME SLEEP. I DON'T MIND STAYING UP BY MYSELF.

BESIDES, AS LONG AS I'M AWAKE, I CAN'T HAVE ANY MORE OF THOSE DREAMS!
DID YOU HAVE ANOTHER WEIRD DREAM?

I HAVEN'T HAD ONE FOR A FEW DAYS NOW, BUT I KEEP WAITING. I'M ALMOST AFRAID TO GO TO SLEEP AT NIGHT!

Y'KNOW, I CAN'T THINK OF A SINGLE DREAM I'VE HAD SINCE I CAME TO THIS VALLEY.
NOT ONE? DO YOU USUALLY REMEMBER YOUR DREAMS?

I **ALWAYS** REMEMBER MY DREAMS!
HMM. WELL, THINGS ARE A LOT **DIFFERENT** HERE THAN THEY ARE IN **BONEVILLE!** MAYBE YOU JUST NEED SOME TIME TO **ADJUST**.

ME?! **BOY! I'LL** TELL YA WHO NEEDS TO DO A LITTLE **ADJUSTING! PHONEY BONE!**
WHY? HE'S FINALLY STARTING TO **FIT IN** AROUND HERE! AT LEAST HE'S STOPPED COMPLAINING ABOUT HIS **CHORES!**

THAT JUST MEANS HE'S **UP TO SOMETHIN'!** HE NEVER **LEARNS!**
YOU'RE TOO HARD ON HIM. BACK WHERE **YOU'RE** FROM, PHONEY WAS **WEALTHY!** IMAGINE WHAT IT MUST BE LIKE TO FIND YOURSELF IN A PLACE WHERE **EVERYTHING** YOU VALUE IS COMPLETELY **WORTHLESS!**

YEAH. PHONEY SURE LOVED HIS **MONEY!** WHAT I WOULDN'T HAVE GIVEN TO **SEE HIS FACE** WHEN HE FOUND OUT YOU DON'T **USE** MONEY HERE!

HEH. HIS **JAW** MUST'VE HIT TH' **FLOOR** WHEN HE FIGURED OUT YOUR WHOLE **ECONOMY** IS BASED ON **POULTRY PRODUCTS!**
HE SEEMS TO HAVE ADJUSTED WELL.

YOU'RE **RIGHT!** A LITTLE HONEST WORK, AND **CLEAN, SIMPLE LIVING** WILL DO HIM **GOOD!**
HI, GUYS!

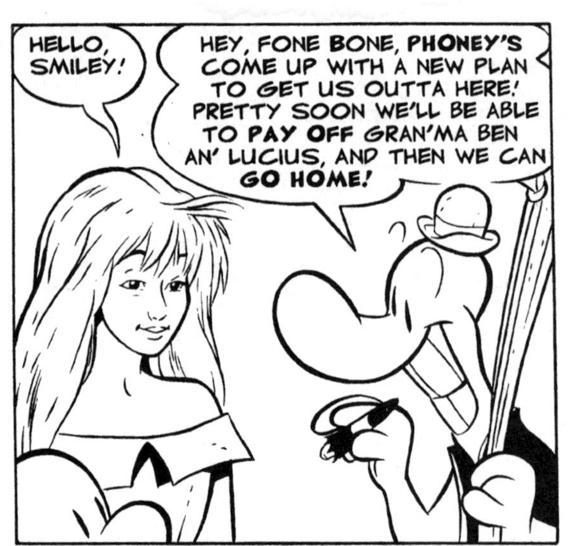
HELLO, SMILEY!
HEY, FONE BONE, PHONEY'S COME UP WITH A NEW PLAN TO GET US OUTTA HERE! PRETTY SOON WE'LL BE ABLE TO PAY OFF GRAN'MA BEN AN' LUCIUS, AND THEN WE CAN GO HOME!

WHAT TH' HECK IS TAKIN' YOU SO LONG?! C'MON! C'MON! YOU GOT ANY IDEA HOW HARD IT IS TO GET 'EM TO SIT IN THOSE LITTLE CHAIRS?!!

ALL SET!

I MISS THAT OL' THRILL...
GIMME GIMME GIMME! EGGS! EGGS! EGGS! I'LL BE RICH!

HEE HEE HEE HEE HEE HEE HEE HEE YES!
OH, YEAH. HE'S ADJUSTED WELL.
I COULD BE WRONG . . .

DID YOU HEAR THAT? THERE'S SOMEONE OUT THERE! WE'VE BEEN CAUGHT!
HOLD ON! HOLD ON! I'LL TAKE A LOOK!

WELL?
ALL CLEAR.

ARE YOU SURE? I THOUGHT I HEARD SOMETHING MOVING UP THERE!
WOULD YOU RELAX? NOBODY IS GOING TO FIND US! QUIT BEIN' SO JUMPY!

WELL, YOU'D BE JUMPY, TOO, IF YOU'D BEEN HIDING IN A HOLE IN TH' GROUND FOR FOUR DAYS!
I HAVE BEEN HIDING IN A HOLE IN TH' GROUND FOR FOUR DAYS! NOW, GO TO SLEEP!

I CAN'T! I HAVE THIS FEELING THAT WE'RE BEING WATCHED!
PROMISE ME YOU'LL KEEP CHECKING!
I HAVEN'T STOPPED CHECKING IN FOUR DAYS!! WHY DON'T YOU CHECK FOR A WHILE?!

OKAY, I WILL!

BUT IF THERE'S SOMEONE OUT THERE, IT WAS YOU WHO STARTED THAT RIOT AT THE COW RACE!
YOU'RE A PAIN IN TH' BUTT, YOU KNOW THAT?

WASN'T ANYBODY OUT THERE, WAS THERE?

NO. BUT THERE COULD'VE BEEN.
KINGDOK WILL NEVER FIND US! WE'RE SAFE HERE! NOW SHUT-UP AND GO TO SLEEP!

I CAN'T SLEEP! MY NERVES ARE SHOT! AND IT'S ALL BECAUSE OF YOU!
YOUR NERVES ARE SHOT BECAUSE YOU'RE A PAIN IN TH' BUTT!

DON'T YOU TAKE THAT TONE OF VOICE WITH ME!
PAIN IN TH' BUTT! PAIN IN TH' BUTT!

Shh!
I HEARD SOMETHING! GO UP AN' LOOK!
AGAIN?! YOU JUST LOOKED!

PLEASE! PLEASE GO CHECK!
ALL RIGHT. ALL RIGHT.

THERE! SATISFIED?! THERE'S NO ONE OUT HERE!

NOW, GO TO SLEEP, YOU BIG, FAT PAIN IN TH' ----

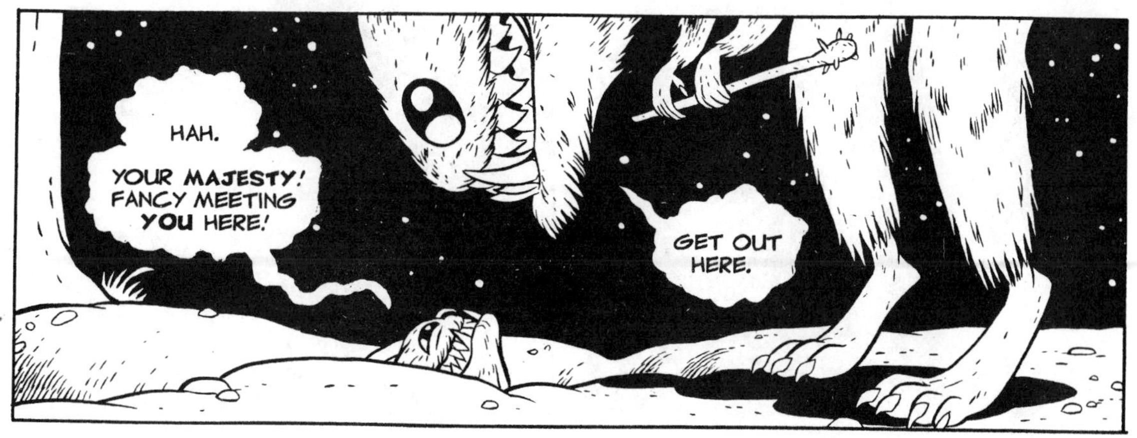
HAH.
YOUR MAJESTY! FANCY MEETING YOU HERE!
GET OUT HERE.

KINGDOK! IT WAS HIS IDEA! I TRIED TO STOP HIM!
IT WAS AN ACCIDENT, SIRE! WE DIDN'T MEAN TO UPSET THE VALLEY CREATURES' COW RACE!

I SHOULD KILL YOU BOTH . . .

BUT YOU KNOW WHAT? I HATE THE FLAT-LANDERS, AND I HATE THE OLD COW WOMAN, AND I REALLY HATE THOSE STUPID COW RACES!
FOR ONCE, YOU TWO MESSED UP, AND I'M HAPPY ABOUT IT!

TH - THEN . . . YOU'RE NOT GOING TO KILL US?
YOU MAY LIVE.
BUT- - BUT WHAT ABOUT TH' HOODED ONE? WE WERE UNDER ORDERS TO LAY LOW!

AM I NOT KINGDOK?! I WILL DISCIPLINE MY TROOPS THE WAY I SEE FIT!!

TAKE THIS!

IT'S A SACK FULL OF RABBITS!
THOUGHT YOU MIGHT ENJOY A GOOD, HOT **MEAL** TONIGHT! THEY'RE ALL SKINNED AN' EVERYTHING!

HEH, HEH, HEH.
GOOD JOB, BOYS! CARRY ON!

WHAT ARE YOU DOING?
I AM LEARNING TO PLAY. THE RED DRAGON IS TEACHING ME.
HE IS A GOOD TEACHER.
AND YOU ARE PRACTICING. YOU ARE A GOOD PUPIL.

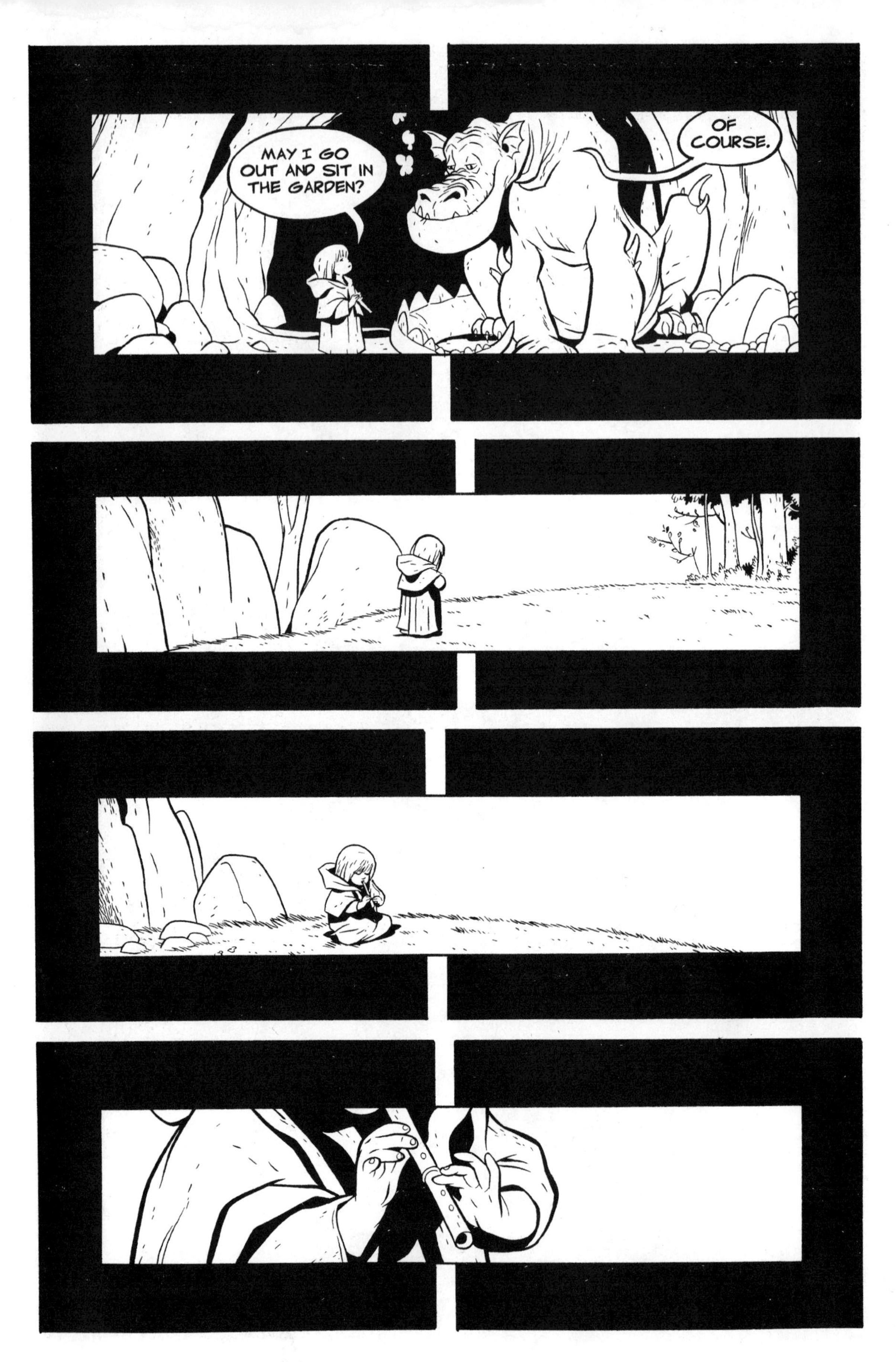
MAY I GO OUT AND SIT IN THE GARDEN?
OF COURSE.

THORN?

YES?
COME TO ME, DEAR . . . . . I AM WAITING.

WHERE ARE YOU? I CAN NOT SEE YOU.
YOU WILL . . . STEP A LITTLE CLOSER . . .

GOOD GIRL . . .
. . . YOU SEE? I HAVE . . . COME FOR YOU . . .
. . . TOUCH ME . . .

NO, NO, NO....
DO NOT BE FRIGHTENED....
..CLOSER... I CAN NOT REACH YOU ...

...ONE TOUCH...
..ONE LITTLE TOUCH....

...AND WE WILL BE TOGETHER

PRINCESS!

BAM
KICK

WHOA.

SNRK. SNORT.

Next: MOBY BONE

BONE™
THAR SHE BLOWS! THERE! THERE!
SHE BLOWS!
THERE GO TH' FLUKES!
IS IT TH' WHITE WHALE?!
YES!
WHERE-A-AWAY, ISHMAEL?
ON TH' LEE-BEAM! TWO MILES OFF!
BUT, PHONEY! MY NAME'S NOT ISHMAEL!
WE DON'T WANT HIM TO GET AWAY, MR. ISHMAEL! LOWER TH' BOATS!

PHONEY BONE! DON'T YOU RECOGNIZE ME? IT'S ME! FONE BONE!
WHEN YER ON MY SHIP, YE'LL ADDRESS ME AS CAPTAIN AHAB! NOW HELP ME GET THIS BOAT OVER TH' SIDE!

THIS ISN'T A BOAT! IT'S A COFFIN!
IT'S HIM! IT'S MOBY DICK! WHERE'S MY LANCE?
PEQUOD
HAR!

PHONEY! STOP! THAT'S NOT MOBY DICK! IT'S SMILEY BONE!
WHAT ARE YOU DOING?!
ARRRR!

GOT HIM!
HANG ON, LAD! WE'RE GOIN' FER TH' RIDE OF OUR LIVES!
PEQUOD

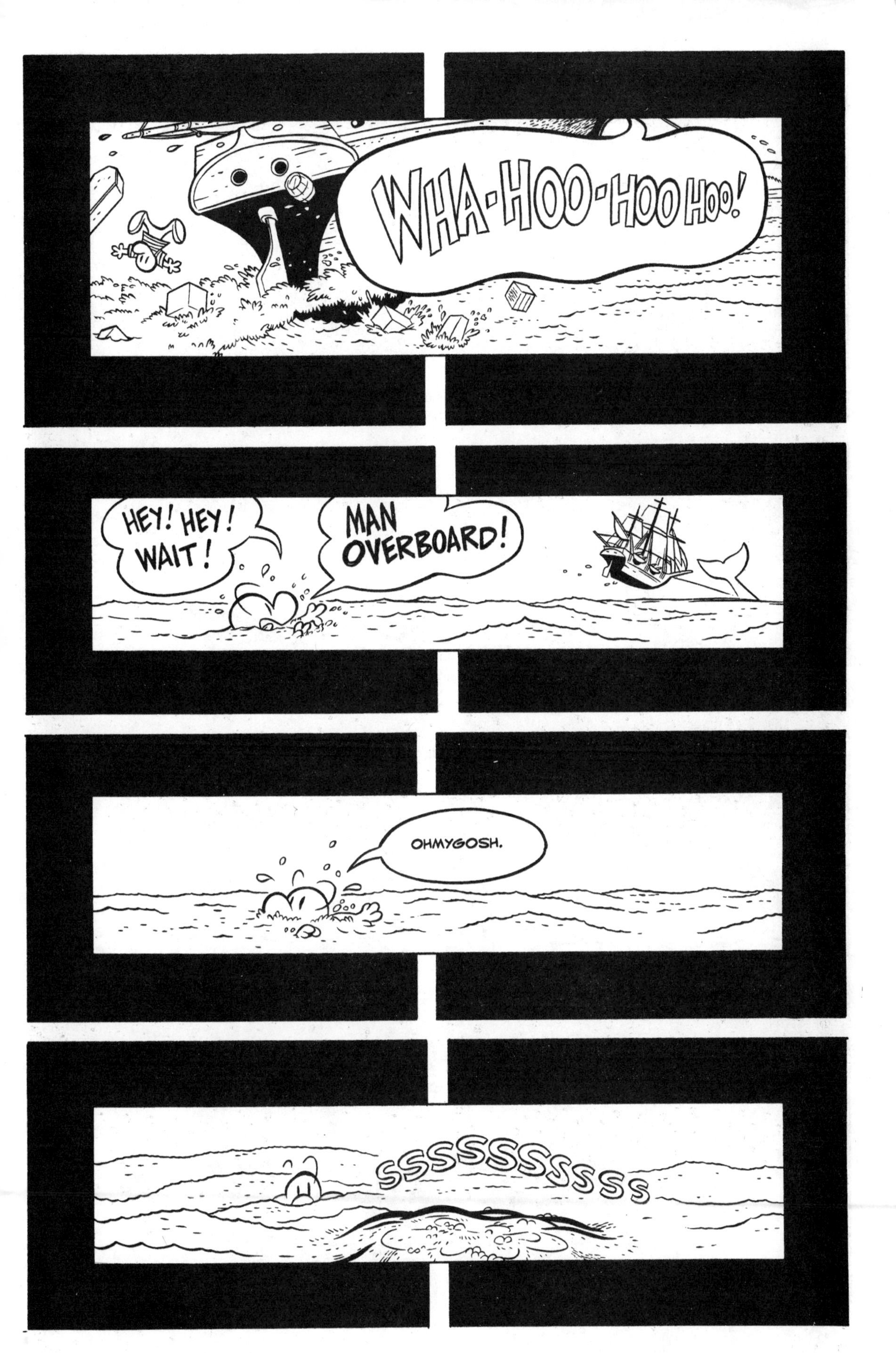
WHA-HOO-HOO HOO!
HEY! HEY! WAIT!
MAN OVERBOARD!
OHMYGOSH.
SSSSSSSSSSS

BAWHOOSH!
PHONEY!
COME BACK!! DON'T LEAVE MEEE!

PLEASE. DON'T LEAVE ME . . .

MMMMM.
SNRK!
SNRK!

UNH.

WHOA.
WHERE AM I?

JEEZ! TH' SUN'S BEEN UP FOR HOURS!

UH, OH! I OVERSLEPT!
WONDER WHERE EVERYBODY IS? PHONEY?

HELLO?
GRAN'MA? THORN?

HMMM. MUST BE OUT AN' ABOUT ALREADY!

HELLO?

HUH! NOBODY'S AROUND!
HIYA, BONE!

HEY, TED!
HOW YOU DOIN', YOU OL' BUG, YOU?
PURTY GOOD! HOW 'BOUTS YOU? BEEN WORKIN' ON YER LOVE POETRYS FOR THORN?

YEAH. I'M NOT A VERY GOOD POET, THOUGH.
BOY! I'LL SAY! I READ THAT ONE YOU LEFT IN TH' FOREST!
"UPON YOUR FEET YOU HAS TEN TOES, THEY LOOKS JES LIKE PO-TA-TOES!"
PEE-YEW!

THAT ONE DOESN'T COUNT! THE RAT CREATURES INTERRUPTED ME!
YOU OUGHTA THANK 'EM! THEY DID YOU A FLAVOR!

I'LL BE SURE TO MENTION IT, NEXT TIME THEY TRY TO EAT ME!
AN' DON'T WORRY BOUT NO ONE ELSE READIN' THAT LOVE POETY! I TORE THAT STINKER UP TO KINGDOM COME!

OKAY, OKAY.
I GET TH' IDEA.
SO WHAT'RE YOU DOIN' HERE, INSTEAD OF DOWN AT TH' SPRINGS 'FETCHIN' FRESH WATER WITH THORN?

WELL, I KINDA OVERSLEPT. I WASN'T SURE WHERE EVERYBODY WAS!
GRANNY AN' LUCIUS IS PLOWIN' UP TH' BACK FIELD, AN' THORN IS DOWN GETTIN' WATER, AN' YER COUSINS IS OFF SOMEWHERES TAKIN' A BREAK!

A BREAK? IS IT LUNCHTIME ALREADY?
HEY, TH' DAY'S HALF OVER, BONE! GET WITH IT, MAN!

WELL, I'SE OFF! A BUG'S DAY IS CHOCK FULL OF IMPORTANT LITTLE DETAILS TO ATTEND TO! SEE YA, BONEY!
BREAKTIME! OH, BOY! I'LL GET MY STUFF AN' WORK ON MY NEW POEM FOR THORN!

NOW TO FIND A NICE, **QUIET** SPOT TO WRITE!

PREFERABLY SOME PLACE **PRIVATE!**

THIS LOOKS GOOD! A SUN DRENCHED MEADOW **BESPECKLED** WITH **WILD FLOWERS**, AN' TH' **AIR** FILLED WITH **WAFTED SCENTS** OF **HONEYSUCKLE** AN' **MARIGOLDS!**

YEAH, YEAH! THIS IS TH' **PERFECT** PLACE TO WORK ON MY **ULTIMATE** EXPRESSION OF LOVE FOR THORN! LET'S SEE . . . A **ROSE** IS A ROSE IS A . . . HUM TE DUM . . .
. . . A **ROSE!** RIGHT!

HMM, HMM, MMMM. HMMM.
OH, **YES!** THIS IS GOOD! THIS IS **REAL** GOOD!
I WONDER WHAT RHYMES WITH **SMOOTH, BROWN THIGH?**

HI, FONE BONE! WHATCHA WORKIN' ON?

NUTHIN'!
UH . . .
NEED SOME HELP WITH THAT WATER?
NO, THAT'S OKAY. I'VE GOT IT . . .

SO . . . DO YOU REMEMBER YOUR DREAM?
WHAT?

YESTERDAY YOU TOLD ME YOU COULDN'T REMEMBER A SINGLE DREAM YOU'VE HAD SINCE COMING TO THE VALLEY - - WELL, THIS MORNING WHEN I SAW YOU WERE HAVING A DREAM,
I LET YOU SLEEP IN!

OH!
YEAH! I DID HAVE A DREAM!
WHAT WAS IT ABOUT?

UM . . . IT WAS WEIRD! I WAS ON A SHIP - -
AN' RIGHT BEFORE I WOKE UP, THE DRAGON ROSE UP OUT OF TH' OCEAN! AN' HE WAS BIG!

I MEAN HUGE! LIKE A MOUNTAIN! AN' HE WAS LOOKIN' AT ME WITH THESE REALLY INTENSE EYES!
I HAD A STRANGE VISITOR IN MY DREAMS LAST NIGHT, TOO! AND HE LOOKED LIKE YOU!

REALLY? YOU HAD A DREAM ABOUT ME?
IT LOOKED LIKE YOU, BUT IT DIDN'T FEEL LIKE YOU. I DON'T THINK OUR TWO DREAMS ARE A COINCIDENCE!

I CAN'T BELIEVE IT!! YOU HAD A DREAM ABOUT ME! HEE HEE HEE!
WE SHOULD TALK ABOUT THIS TONIGHT, OKAY?

OKAY! GOSH! WHAT WAS TH' DREAM ABOUT? IF YOU DON'T MIND ME ASKIN'?

WAIT! BEFORE YOU TELL ME! HERE! HAVE SOME VIOLETS! THEY'LL LOOK SO LOVELY NEXT TO YOUR EYES!

HOO, HEE... I HOPE YOU DON'T THINK I'M BEING TOO FORWARD...
NOT AT ALL.

MY, WHAT A BEAUTIFUL BARITONE VOICE YOU HAVE.
DON'T YOU THINK DAISIES WOULD HAVE SET OFF MY EYES BETTER?

SIGH.
LOVE LIFE HASN'T **IMPROVED** MUCH, HAS IT?

NO. NOT THAT IT'S ANY OF YOUR **BUSINESS**!
FAIR ENOUGH. I'LL BE ON MY WAY.

HEY, WAIT A MINUTE, DRAGON! YOU GOTTA HEAR ABOUT THIS **DREAM** I HAD LAST NIGHT! **YOU** WERE **IN** IT!

I SAW THIS GIANT IMAGE OF YOUR **HEAD**! YOU DIDN'T **SAY** ANYTHING-- YOU WERE JUST **STARIN'** AT ME! WHAT DO YOU THINK? YOU THINK IT'S **WEIRD** THAT I'D HAVE A DREAM LIKE THAT?
NO.

THORN HAD AN **INTRUDER** IN HER DREAMS LAST NIGHT.
SO DID YOU.

WELCOME ABOARD, ISHMAEL.

HEY, YOU! NOW JUST A MINUTE--- DON'T YOU ISHMAEL ME!!

YOU---! YOU---!

STAY OUTTA MY DREAMS!

I MEAN IT!!

MAN!
THAT IS SPOOKY! THAT IS REALLY SPOOKY!

HOW TH' HECK DID HE KNOW I WAS ISHMAEL IN THAT DREAM? THAT'S IMPOSSIBLE! IT'S A COINCIDENCE!

DON'T THINK ABOUT IT.
NOW, WHERE WAS I?

A ROSE IS A ROSE IS A ROSE . . .

OH, YEAH! MY MASTERPIECE!
HMM, HMM.

HOWDY, FONE BONE! FINALLY GOT UP, I SEE!
HEY, GUYS. WHATCHA UP TO?

AS LITTLE AS WE CAN GET AWAY WITH! WHAT'RE YOU DOIN'? WRITIN' SOMETHIN'?
ME?
NO.
LEMME SEE THAT!

HEY!
WELL. WELL, WHAT HAVE WE HERE? POETRY! MISSIVES OF LOVE TO OUR DEAR, AND INCREDIBLY GOOD LOOKING FRIEND THORN!

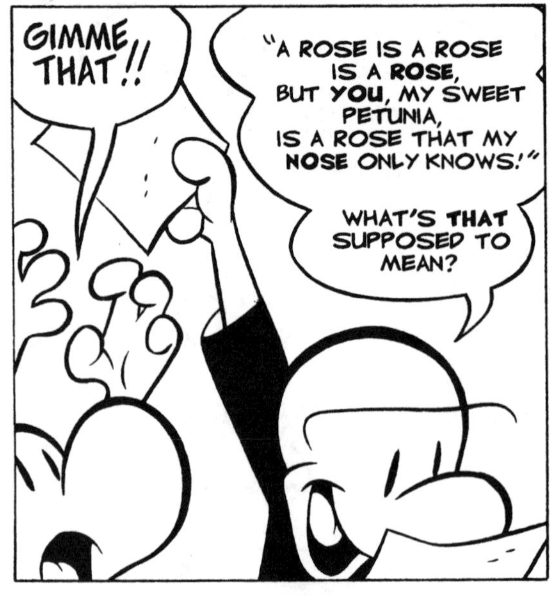
GIMME THAT!!
"A ROSE IS A ROSE IS A ROSE, BUT YOU, MY SWEET PETUNIA, IS A ROSE THAT MY NOSE ONLY KNOWS!"
WHAT'S THAT SUPPOSED TO MEAN?

IT RHYMES!
FONE BONE, FONE BONE, FONE BONE! WRITIN' LOVE POEMS TO A GIRL, HUH? HOW MANY OF THESE THINGS HAVE YOU WRITTEN TO HER?

A COUPLE HUNDRED.
JEEZ! THORN MUST THINK YOU'RE A DROOLING IDIOT BY NOW!

SHE DOES NOT!!

I NEVER SHOWED 'EM TO HER.
WIMP!

YOU'RE LETTIN' THESE WOMEN-FOLK GET TO YA, FONE BONE!
WHAT DO YOU MEAN?

I SEE HOW YOU JUMP WHENEVER THORN WANTS YOU TO DO SOMETHING!
OH, FONE BONE, HELP ME CARRY THE WATER! OH, FONE BONE, IT'S TIME TO DO TH' LAUNDRY!

PHONEY! GRAN'MA BEN AND THORN ARE GIVING US A PLACE TO LIVE! WE HAVE TO HELP OUT WITH TH' CHORES!

OH, YEAH? WELL, YOU DON'T SEE ME AN' SMILEY DROP EVERYTHING AN' GO RUNNIN' EVERY TIME THORN AN' GRAN'MA BEN SNAP THEIR FINGERS!

DING! DING! DING! DING!
OBOY!
IT'S TH' DINNER BELL!
HANG ON, GRAN'MA! WE'RE COMIN'!

HOLD IT, BOYS! NOT IN TH' HOUSE! I WANT YA BACK IN TH' YARD WITH ME!
OOF!
WHAM!
OW!

WHAT GIVES, GRAN'MA?
YEAH, WHAT'S GOIN' ON? IT'S WAY TOO EARLY FOR DINNER!

I DIDN'T CALL YA TO EAT DINNER, YA IDIOTS! I WANT YA TO MAKE DINNER!
SEE? WHAT'D I TELL YOU? WOMEN AIN'T NOTHIN' BUT TROUBLE!

FILL THIS KETTLE WITH WATER AND BRING IT BACK TO TH' CHICKEN COOP! AN' BUILD A FIRE UNDER IT. I NEED THAT WATER BOILIN', YOU GOT THAT?
YES, M'AM!

YOU TWO COME WITH ME.

I WANT YOU BOYS TO CATCH YOURSELVES FOUR CHICKENS! WHEN SMILEY'S GOT THAT WATER GOIN' NICE AN' HOT, DIP TH' BIRDS IN IT! I WANT EVERY ONE OF THEM FEATHERS GONE, SO SOAK 'EM GOOD! I BETTER BE SMELLIN' WET FEATHERS BACK HERE!

POO! THERE'S A SMELL YOU DON'T FORGET TOO QUICK!
OHMYGOSH.
WE'RE GONNA BOIL 'EM ALIVE?!

OF COURSE NOT, DEAR. YOU'RE GONNA CUT THEIR HEADS OFF FIRST.
WITH WHAT?

WITH TH' HATCHET.
UH . . .
ARE THEY GONNA . . . Y'KNOW . . . RUN AROUND TH' YARD? SQUIRTIN' BLOOD AN' STUFF?

WHAT'S TH' MATTER? AIN'T YOU BOYS EVER CHOPPED TH' HEAD OFF A CHICKEN BEFORE?
UH . . .
UH . . .

OH, FER HEAVEN'S SAKES! IF YA CAN'T HANDLE A LITTLE FLAPPIN' AROUND, JUST GRAB TH' CHICKEN BY TH' NECK AN' GIVE HER A GOOD CRANK OVER YOUR HEAD -- THAT'LL KILL HER FIRST!

NEXT: ROAD TRIP!

BONK
ALL RIGHT, YOU LAZY BONES! WAKE IT UP!
WE'RE HEADIN' BACK TO BARRELHAVEN, AN' I WANNA GET AN EARLY START!
TODAY?! RIGHT NOW? AW, JEEZ! IT'S STILL DARK OUT!
WE'RE GOIN' FOR A RIDE?!
THAT'S RIGHT! ALL TH' CHORES ARE DONE - - ALL THE SPRING PLANTING'S DONE - - AND YOU KNOW WHAT THAT MEANS! YOU TWO ARE COMIN' WITH ME TO START WORKIN' OFF THAT 100 TO 1 LONGSHOT BET!
AS OF THIS MOMENT, YOU BOYS ARE MINE!
I HATE IT WHEN HE DOES THAT.

THIS IS ALL YOUR FAULT, YOU KNOW. IF YOU'D WON THAT STUPID COW RACE I'D BE RICH RIGHT NOW, INSTEAD OF WASHIN' DISHES FOR BIGFOOT! OVER THERE!
NOBODY ASKED YOU TO CLIMB INTO TH' COW SUIT WITH ME.

WHAT ELSE WAS I GONNA DO?! I CAN'T TRUST YOU TO DO ANYTHING RIGHT!!
BALLAST! THAT'S ALL YOU WERE!
B-A-L-A-S-S-T!

KNOCK IT OFF! YOU TWO BETTER NOT CRAP AROUND LIKE THIS TH' WHOLE WAY TO BARRELHAVEN! NOW, C'MON, LET'S GO!
YEAH, YEAH. ARE WE GONNA EAT BREAKFAST FIRST, OR WHAT?

WE'LL EAT ON TH' ROAD.
HAPPINESS ABOUNDING!
ROAD RATIONS!
I LOVE THOSE HARD, STALE, STUFFED BREAD THINGIES!

HOW DID YOU SLEEP LAST NIGHT, FONE BONE?
I DIDN'T HAVE ANY MORE WEIRD DREAMS. WHAT ABOUT YOU?

EVERYBODY OUTSIDE! MOVE IT! MOVE IT!
I SLEPT PRETTY HARD. NO NEW DREAMS FOR ME, EITHER.
RRRR.

GOOD MORNING, EVERYONE! MY! DON'T **WE** LOOK BRIGHT AND **BUSHY-TAILED!**
WE'RE ALL READY TO GO, ROSIE.
HEY, GRAN'MA! DID YOU PACK ANY OF THOSE HARD, LITTLE, STUFFED **BREAD THINGIES** FOR ME?

OF COURSE, DEAR. I MADE THEM **TWO DAYS** AGO, SO THEY'D BE **EXTRA** STALE - - JUST TH' WAY YOU LIKE 'EM!
YES!
RRRR.

WHAT DO YOU THINK, ROSE? IS TH' WEATHER GONNA HOLD?
IT'S TOO EARLY TO SAY. IT MAY RAIN BEFORE YOU GET TO TH' VILLAGE.

BETTER GET STARTED THEN.
OKAY! TIME TO GO!

PHONEY! YOU AND SMILEY BONE GET IN TH' CART. WHAT ABOUT **YOU**, FONE BONE? YOU WANNA STAY WITH ME AN' THORN, OR GO WITH YOUR **COUSINS**?
I GET TO **CHOOSE**?

YES, YOU GET TO CHOOSE! YOU DIDN'T BET ON TH' COW RACE! YOU'RE WELCOME TO STAY HERE ON TH' FARM WITH US!
WELL . . . . I GUESS YOU COULD USE MY HELP WITH SOME OF THE CHORES. BEING WITH THORN IS GOOD - -
I MEAN, YOU AND THORN! I MEAN I'LL STAY WITH BOTH OF YOU!
GEE. WHAT A SURPRISE!

GOOD BYE, BOYS! KEEP A SHARP LOOK OUT ON TH' ROAD!
WE'LL BE BACK IN A FEW DAYS, ROSE. TAKE CARE OF YOURSELF.

SEE YA LATER, GUYS!
BITE ME.

I'VE GOT A FEW THINGS TO FINISH UP BEFORE BREAKFAST. YOU TWO KNOW WHAT YOU'RE GONNA DO TODAY?
I WAS THINKING ABOUT STARTING UP A GARDEN OUT BY THE WELL.

THAT'S A FINE IDEA! BUT FEED TH' CHICKENS FIRST!
OKAY! C'MON, FONE BONE!

LET'S PLAY A GAME!
NO.

LET'S TALK ABOUT YOU!
NO.
AND GET THAT CIGAR OUTTA MY FACE!

CAN WE EAT NOW?
NO.
ARE WE THERE YET?
NO.
YOU A WIDOWER?
NO.
EVER BEEN MARRIED?
NO.

I ALMOST GOT MARRIED ONCE.

REALLY?!
IT WAS A LONG TIME AGO. . . . SHE WAS A BEAUTIFUL WOMAN - - TH' MOST BEAUTIFUL WOMAN IN TH' WHOLE VALLEY . . .

WE WERE IN LOVE, AND WE COURTED. A LOT OF FOLKS THOUGHT WE WERE GONNA GET HITCHED . . .

SO WHAT HAPPENED? WHY DIDN'T YOU GET MARRIED?

SHE DIDN'T WANT TO.
HMM. THAT STORM IS BLOWIN' IN A LOT FASTER THAN I THOUGHT.

UH, OH!
WE GOT TROUBLE!

THERE'S SOMEONE FOLLOWING US!

WHERE? I DON'T SEE ANYTHING!
IT WENT INTO TH' BUSHES! IT WAS A RAT CREATURE!

ARE YOU SURE? MAYBE IT WAS TH' WIND BLOWIN' TH' BUSHES AROUND . . .
HEY!
I THOUGHT GRAN'MA BEN SAID IT WAS SAFE TO MAKE THIS TRIP!!

ROSE ISN'T ALWAYS RIGHT. WE'RE FAR ENOUGH AWAY FROM TH' DRAGON'S PROTECTION THAT THEY MIGHT ATTACK US . . .
. . . BUT THAT MEANS WE'RE CUT OFF! WE HAVE TO MAKE IT TO TH' VILLAGE ON OUR OWN!

SMILEY! GET OUT AND RIDE TH' EXTRA COW - - IF WE HAVE TO MAKE A RUN FOR IT, WE NEED TO LIGHTEN UP TH' CART!

I FELT A DROP!
I THINK TH' STORM IS GONNA START!
HERE IT COMES!
RUN FOR THE BARN!

KRAK BOOM!

WHOA! WE GOT CREAMED!
IT ONLY RAINED ON US FOR A MOMENT, AND I'M SOAKED!

LET'S SIT DOWN.
I LOVE BEING IN THE BARN WHEN IT STORMS.

LISTEN TO ALL THE DROPS HITTING THE ROOF.
LOOK OUTSIDE! IT'S LIKE NIGHT OUT THERE!

I HOPE PHONEY AND SMILEY ARE OKAY.
A LITTLE RAIN WON'T HURT THEM.

I WASN'T THINKING ABOUT THE RAIN.

I'M SURE THEY'RE SAFE. LUCIUS WILL PROTECT THEM . . .

. . . OR THE DRAGON WILL.

WELL, C'MON. THERE'S SOMETHING WE HAVE TO DO.
THERE IS?

IT'S TIME TO TALK ABOUT THE **DREAMS** . . .

KREEEEEEK
GROOANN
YOU LOOK A LITTLE **NERVOUS**, BONE.
I DON'T KNOW WHAT'S **WORSE!** WAITIN' FOR TH' **RAT CREATURES**, OR WAITIN' FOR TH' **WIND** TO BLOW A **TREE** DOWN ON OUR **HEADS!**

DON'T WORRY ABOUT TH' **TREES**. THEY'VE STOOD UP TO WORSE THAN **THIS** - -
CRACK

R-R-R-R-R-R-R-R-R-R
SSHHHSHS
SNAP!
CRAK!

CRASSH!
OH, YEAH?! THAT WAS A **TREE** FALLIN' **DOWN** SOMEWHERE! AN' **CLOSE**, TOO! WORRIED ABOUT IT **NOW**, MR. SMARTY PANTS?

THAT TREE WAS UP AHEAD.
SOMEBODY JUST BLOCKED OUR PATH.
LUCIUS!

WHAT DO I DO? WHAT DO I DO?
WALK YOUR COW OVER TO US . . . BUT DO IT SLOWLY. DON'T MAKE ANY SUDDEN MOVES.

HERE. TAKE THIS KNIFE AN' KEEP YER HEAD DOWN. . . I'M GONNA TRY TO STALL 'EM SO SMILEY CAN GET PAST US . . .

HAIRY MEN!
WHY HAVE YOU STOPPED US?!
SSSSSSSSSS

SSSSS
GIVE US THE CREATURE . . . . . . WITH THE STAR ON ITS CHEST . . .

. . . GIVE IT TO US . . . . . AND WE WILL LET YOU GO ON YOUR WAY . . . .

SMILEY! GO!! RUN TO TH' TAVERN - - GET HELP!

TOO LATE!

SMACK

YEEE-HAW!
OOF!
STOP THEM!

THE REINS!
WHAT?

GET TH' REINS!!

BAM!

CRUNCH

OH, NO!
WHAT?! WHAT?!

OLD MAN'S CAVE!!

YIP! YIP! YIP!

YIP! YIP! YIP! YIP!

WOO! WOO!

SMILEY! YOU SAVED US!
YAH HOO!

SMILEY! THE CLIFF!!

I'M WITH YA!
GIT ALONG LI'L DAWGIE! YAH! YAH!

YAAAAAAAA

AAAAA

GAAH!
SPUT! SPUTTER!

YOU-- YOU-- YOU'RE CRAZY!!
I GOT US AWAY FROM TH' RAT CREATURES, DIDN'T I?

RRRRRRRFF!
YEAH.
YOU DID DO THAT.

KRAK
BOOM!

IS EVERYTHING I DO WITH YOU TWO BOYS GONNA BE LIKE THIS?
LIKE WHAT?

I WONDER WHAT THE COFFIN REPRESENTS . . .
IN YOUR DREAM YOU WERE ISHMAEL.
DID THE COFFIN SYMBOLIZE ANYTHING FOR ISHMAEL IN MOBY DICK?

YEAH, WELL, SURE IT DID IN TH' BOOK. IT STOOD FOR LIFE AND IRONY . . . BUT IT'S NOT TH' MOBY DICK PART OF MY DREAM THAT I'M WORRIED ABOUT!
YOU'RE WORRIED ABOUT THE PART WHERE THE DRAGON JUST STARED AT YOU.

YEAH! AN' I TALKED TO HIM ABOUT IT, TOO! I TOLD HIM HE WAS IN MY DREAM - - BUT I DIDN'T TELL HIM THAT PART OF TH' DREAM WAS ABOUT MOBY DICK . . . I DIDN'T THINK IT WAS IMPORTANT . . .

HE SAID HE KNEW ABOUT THE INTRUDER IN YOUR DREAMS, THORN! BUT NOW I'D HAD AN INTRUDER IN MINE! WITHOUT MISSIN' A BEAT, HE SAYS - - WELCOME ABOARD, ISHMAEL!
JUST LIKE THAT! THEN HE LEFT!

HE SAID ISHMAEL? HE KNEW YOUR DREAM WAS ABOUT MOBY DICK?
SCARY, HUH? HOW'D HE KNOW WHAT I WAS DREAMING ABOUT?
AND HE KNEW ABOUT THAT CREEPY GUY IN YOUR DREAM, TOO! SO WHO WAS THAT?

IN MY DREAM? I DON'T KNOW . . .
HE WORE THAT LONG, DARK HOOD. WHOEVER IT WAS, HE REALLY FRIGHTENED ME.
HM. AND YOU SAID HE HAD MY FACE.

HE HAD YOUR FACE, BUT I THINK . . . HE WAS JUST USING IT TO LURE ME TO HIM.
AND A GROUP OF HOODED PEOPLE WERE TAKING YOU OVER THE MOUNTAINS TO LIVE WITH THE DRAGONS . . .

YES. THAT WAS THE DREAM I USED TO HAVE AS A LITTLE GIRL.
I WONDER HOW SAFE IT IS FOR US TO BE TALKING ABOUT THIS . . .
ALL THE DREAMS ARE ABOUT DRAGONS AND HOODED PEOPLE! THERE'S A PATTERN, HERE, THORN! SOMETHING'S GOING ON!

DID YOU HEAR SOME-THING?
GRAN'MA BEN KNOWS THE TRUTH ABOUT WHERE YOU WERE RAISED! HOW COME SHE'S NEVER TOLD YOU? INSTEAD, SHE TOLD YOU THAT DRAGONS AREN'T REAL - -

CREEAK

Next: Double or Nothing

BONE™
KRAK-KK POW!
GRAN'MA?
ARE YOU ALL RIGHT?
MAN! SHE DOESN'T LOOK TOO GOOD.
GRAN'MA, YOU . . . YOU SCARED US! WE DIDN'T HEAR YOU COME IN THE BARN - -

KEEE-RA-

KKA-BOOM

WHAT TH' HECK WAS **THAT** ALL ABOUT?!
I DON'T KNOW. SHE LOOKED **REALLY** UPSET.
DO YOU THINK SHE OVERHEARD US TALKING ABOUT OUR **DREAMS?**

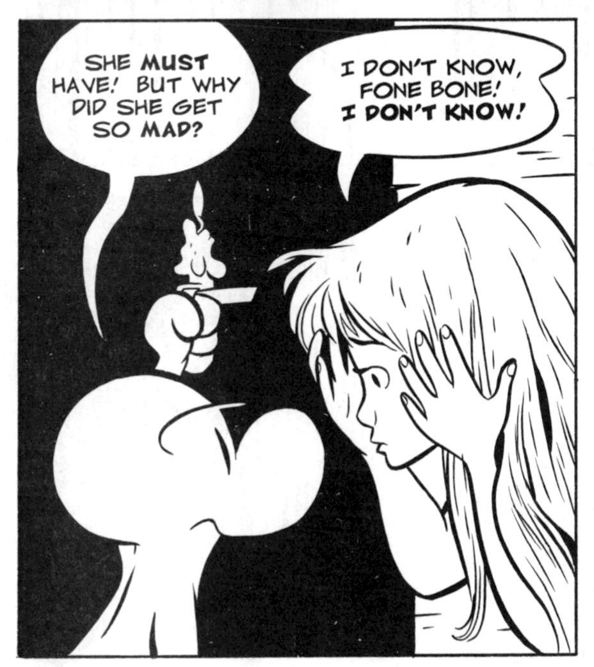
SHE **MUST** HAVE! BUT WHY DID SHE GET SO **MAD?**
I DON'T KNOW, FONE BONE! **I DON'T KNOW!**

WELL, **I** DO! SOMEONE'S BEEN PLAYIN' AROUND IN OUR **HEADS** GIVIN' US **NIGHTMARES**, AN' YOUR **GRANDMOTHER** KNOWS SOMETHIN' **ABOUT IT!**

C'MON! WE GOTTA CATCH HER!

KRACK
BOOM

FONE BONE! WAIT!

SHE'S NOT IN THE HOUSE!
SHE'S GOING INTO THE **WOODS!**

KRAK
YIKES!

BABOOM
WHOA! THAT LIGHTNING WAS CLOSE!

OKAY, I GIVE! LET'S GO BACK TO TH' HOUSE!

I'M GONNA FIND GRAN'MA BEN!
GRAN'MA!
THORN!
WE CAN'T STAY OUT HERE! IT'S TOO DANGEROUS!

WE'LL NEVER FIND HER! WE CAN'T EVEN SEE TWO FEET IN FRONT OF US!

THORN!
STOP!
NO!

SHE WAS HEADED THIS WAY! WE'LL FIND HER!

KRAAKKLE!

GRAN'MA!

YOU SCARED US HALF TO DEATH! ARE YOU OKAY?

GRAN'MA, WHAT ARE YOU DOING?
GO HOME, THORN.

I'M NOT GOING BACK WITHOUT YOU!
AN' I'M NOT GOIN' BACK UNTIL YOU TELL US WHAT'S GOIN' ON!

HOW MUCH DID YOU OVERHEAR OF ME AN' THORN TALKIN' ABOUT OUR DREAMS?

KA-BOOM!

EVERYTHING . . .
I HEARD EVERY-THING.

NOW, YOU TAKE MY GRANDDAUGHTER BACK TO TH' FARMHOUSE WHERE IT'S SAFE, AN' START MINDIN' YOUR OWN BUSINESS, BONE!

I'M NOT BEIN' NOSEY! I'VE BEEN HAVIN' WEIRD DREAMS, TOO! HOW COME YOU'RE ACTIN' LIKE THIS, GRAN'MA?

FIRST YOU COME SNEAKIN' INTO TH' BARN TO LISTEN IN ON OUR CONVERSATION, THEN YOU GO CHARGIN' OFF IN TH' WOODS LIKE A CRAZY PERSON!

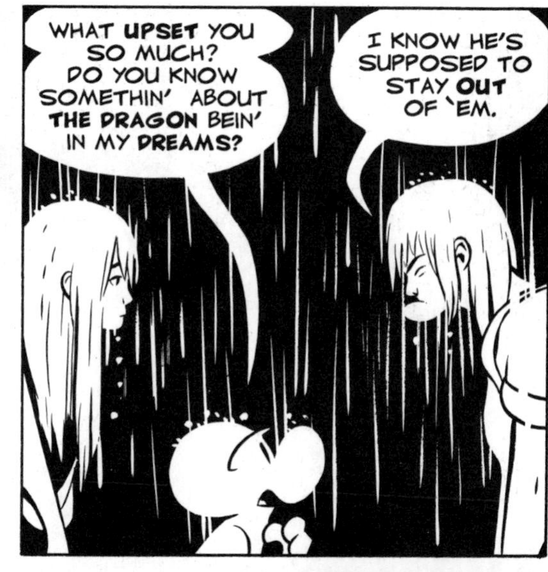
WHAT UPSET YOU SO MUCH? DO YOU KNOW SOMETHIN' ABOUT THE DRAGON BEIN' IN MY DREAMS?
I KNOW HE'S SUPPOSED TO STAY OUT OF 'EM.

WHAT?
GO BACK TO TH' HOUSE! THESE WOODS ARE DANGEROUS!

YOU'RE GOING TO SEE HIM RIGHT NOW, AREN'T YOU? YOU'RE GOING TO SEE THE DRAGON!
WHAT DO YOU MEAN HE'S SUPPOSED TO STAY OUT OF MY DREAMS?

FOR TH' LAST TIME, BONE, GET BACK TO TH' HOUSE BEFORE - -

KEERAAK BOOM!

DID YOU SEE THAT?

I WASN'T LOOKING!
Shh!

RAT CREATURES.
STAY LOW.

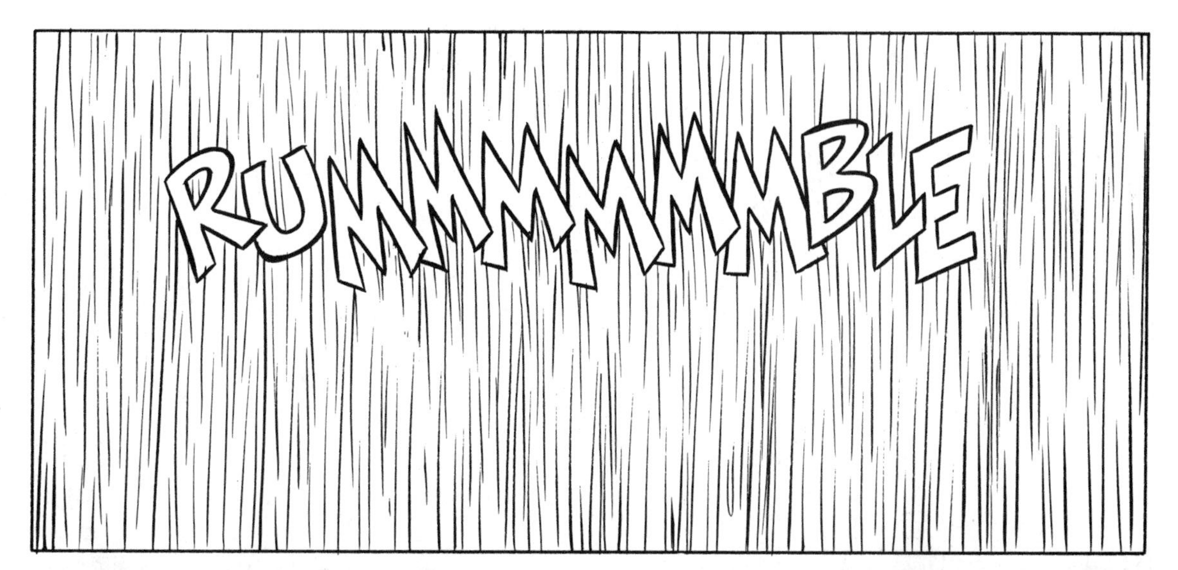
RUMMMMMBLE

ARE WE THERE YET?
NO.
JUST CHECKIN'.
WHOA, HOSS! YAH! EASY BOY!

WHOA! WHOA! GIDDIYUP!

YAH, MULE! YAH! YAH!

CIRCLE TH' WAGONS!!

WE'RE BLAZIN' A NEW TRAIL, BOYS!
IF HE GOES AROUND US ONE MORE TIME, I'M GONNA BLOW . . .

LET'S MAKE CAMP FOR TH' NIGHT! WE'LL SING SONGS, AN' EAT BEANS UNDER TH' STARS!

ARE WE THERE YET?
NO.
JUST CHECKIN'.
YEE-HAW!

SMILEY! GIMME THAT GUITAR!

HEY! THAT'S MY HORSE! LUCIUS, MAKE HIM GIVE ME MY HORSE BACK!
IT'S NOT A HORSE, YOU NUMBSKULL! WHY CAN'T YOU TRUDGE ALONG QUIETLY? TRY TO BE MISERABLE LIKE US!

TH' TROUBLE WITH YOU, PHONEY BONE, IS YOU DON'T KNOW HOW TO HAVE FUN!
TH' TROUBLE WITH ME IS I GOT A BRAIN!

HUH! THAT'S A LAUGH.

OH, IS THAT RIGHT? AN' WHAT MAKES YOU SO SMART?

HE SURE OUTSMARTED YOU AT TH' COW RACE! AN' YOU GOTTA PAY FOR IT BY WASHIN' DISHES AT TH' TAVERN FOR TH' REST OF TH' SUMMER!
DON'T HELP ME. HERE. GO RIDE YOUR HORSE.

OKAY, LUCIUS, I ADMIT YOU CAME OUT ON TOP IN TH' COW RACE, BUT DON'T THINK BRAINS HAD ANYTHING TO DO WITH IT! YOU JUST GOT LUCKY!

I HAD YOU PEGGED FROM TH' VERY BEGINING, SHORT STUFF. FACE IT, MY BRAIN WHIPPED YOUR BRAIN.

OH, YEAH? AND I SUPPOSE WE HAVE YOUR GENIUS TO THANK FOR THIS LITTLE STROLL THROUGH A MONSOON?
ARE YOU SAYIN' THIS IS MY FAULT?!

THIS TRIP SURE WASN'T MY IDEA! WE GOT ATTACKED BY RAT CREATURES, WE LOST OUR COWS, WE LOST OUR CART, AN' WE ALMOST GOT KILLED BECUASE OF YOU!
!

WHY, YOU UNGRATEFUL, LITTLE RUNT! TH' ONLY REASON THE RAT CREATURES ATTACKED US WAS BECAUSE YOU WERE WITH US! I SAVED YOUR BUTT!

TECHNICALLY, I SAVED BOTH YOUR BUTTS!
GO RIDE YOUR HORSE!

YOU MISSED YOUR **BIG CHANCE**, LUCIUS! YOU COULDA HANDED ME OVER TO 'EM! WHY **DIDN'T** YA?
'CAUSE YOU OWE ME A **LOTTA** EGGS . . .

. . . AND I'M **REALLY** LOOKIN' FORWARD TO BUSTIN' YOUR CHOPS ALL **SUMMER** LONG!

YOU'LL BE **THANKIN'** ME BY TH' END OF TH' SUMMER! AT LEAST WITH **ME** THERE, THAT TWO-BIT JOINT HAS A CHANCE TO TURN A PROFIT!
OH! OH!
NOW YOU GOT SOMETHIN' TO SAY ABOUT TH' WAY I RUN MY **BAR?!**

OH, **PLEASE!** DON'T EVEN GET ME **STARTED!**

YOU THINK YOU CAN RUN THE **BARRELHAVEN TAVERN** BETTER THAN **I** CAN?

YOU WOULDN'T KNOW A **BOTTOM-LINE** IF IT JUMPED UP AN' TUGGED YA ON TH' **BEARD!**
CARE TO MAKE A LITTLE **WAGER** ON THAT?

A WAGER? WHAT KIND OF WAGER?
I SAY MY CUSTOMERS LIKE TH' WAY I RUN MY PLACE!

WE'LL SPLIT TH' BAR RIGHT DOWN TH' MIDDLE! YOU TAKE ONE END, AND I'LL TAKE THE OTHER! WE'LL JUST SEE WHO TH' CUSTOMERS LIKE BETTER!

PIECE OF CAKE!
IS IT A BET?

WHAT'RE TH' STAKES?
DOUBLE OR NOTHIN'.

AT TH' NEXT NEW MOON, IF YOUR END OF THE BAR IS MORE POPULAR, YOU'RE OFF TH' HOOK! IF MY END IS, YOU'RE GONNA BE WASHIN' DISHES FOR THE REST OF YOUR LIFE!

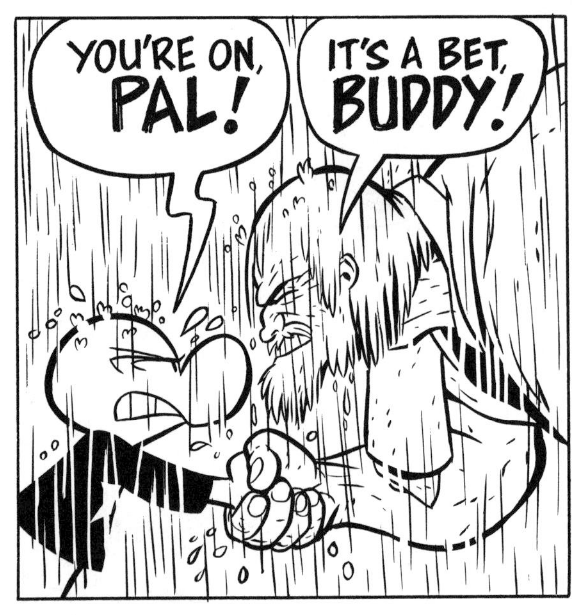
YOU'RE ON, PAL!
IT'S A BET, BUDDY!

I WAS WRONG. YOU DO KNOW HOW TO HAVE FUN!
RRRR.
RRRR.

RRRR.
RRRR.

SO. ARE WE THERE YET?
RRRR.
RRRR.
the Barrel Haven
R. Down Prop.

HEY, EVERYBODY! LOOK! MR. DOWN IS BACK!

IT'S THOSE BONES!
TH' ONES THAT RIGGED TH' COW RACE!

LET'S GET 'EM!

I WAS WRONG. YOU DO KNOW HOW TO HAVE FUN!
RRRR.
RRRR.

RRRR.
RRRR.

SO. ARE WE THERE YET?
RRRR.
RRRR.
the Barrel Haven
L. Down Prop.

HEY, EVERYBODY!
LOOK!
MR. DOWN IS
BACK!

IT'S THOSE BONES!
TH' ONES THAT RIGGED TH' COW RACE!

LET'S GET `EM!

HOLD IT RIGHT THERE!

WHAT DO YOU THINK YOU'RE DOIN'? ME AN' GRAN'MA BEN SETTLED ALL YOUR LOSSES! YOU GOT NO MORE BEEF WITH THESE BOYS!

BESIDES ... THEY'RE MINE!

YOU GOT A LOT OF NERVE SHOWIN' YOUR FACE AROUND HERE AGAIN, BONE!
YEAH! YOU MUST HAVE SOME SORTA DEATH WISH!

ALL RIGHT, EVERYBODY JUST SETTLE DOWN! THESE FELLAS OWE ME A LOTTA EGGS -- THEY'RE GONNA BE WORKIN' HERE FOR AWHILE, SO START GETTIN' USED TO IT!

JONATHAN! SET EVERYBODY UP WITH A ROUND ON TH' HOUSE!

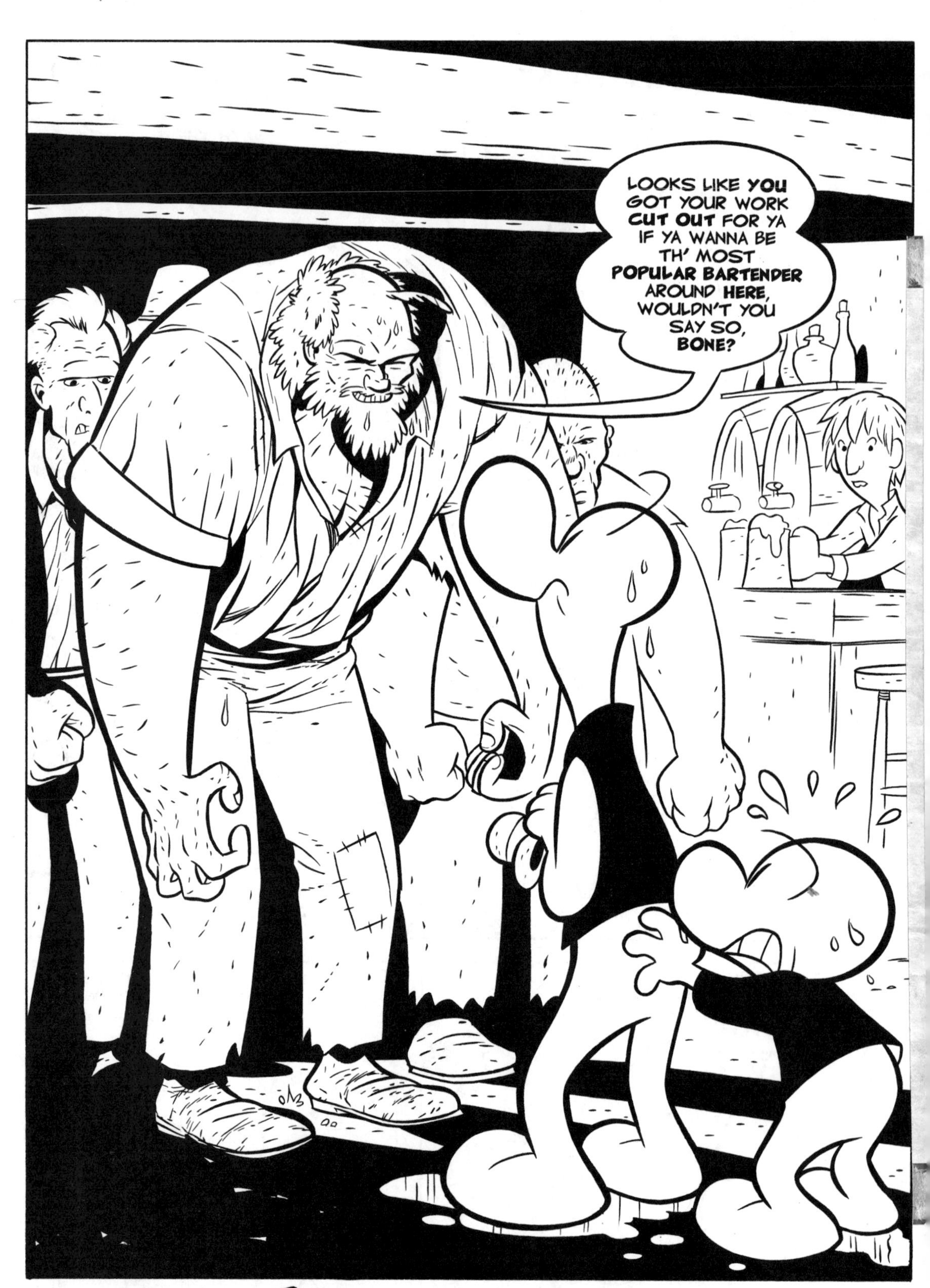

NEXT: EYES OF THE STORM

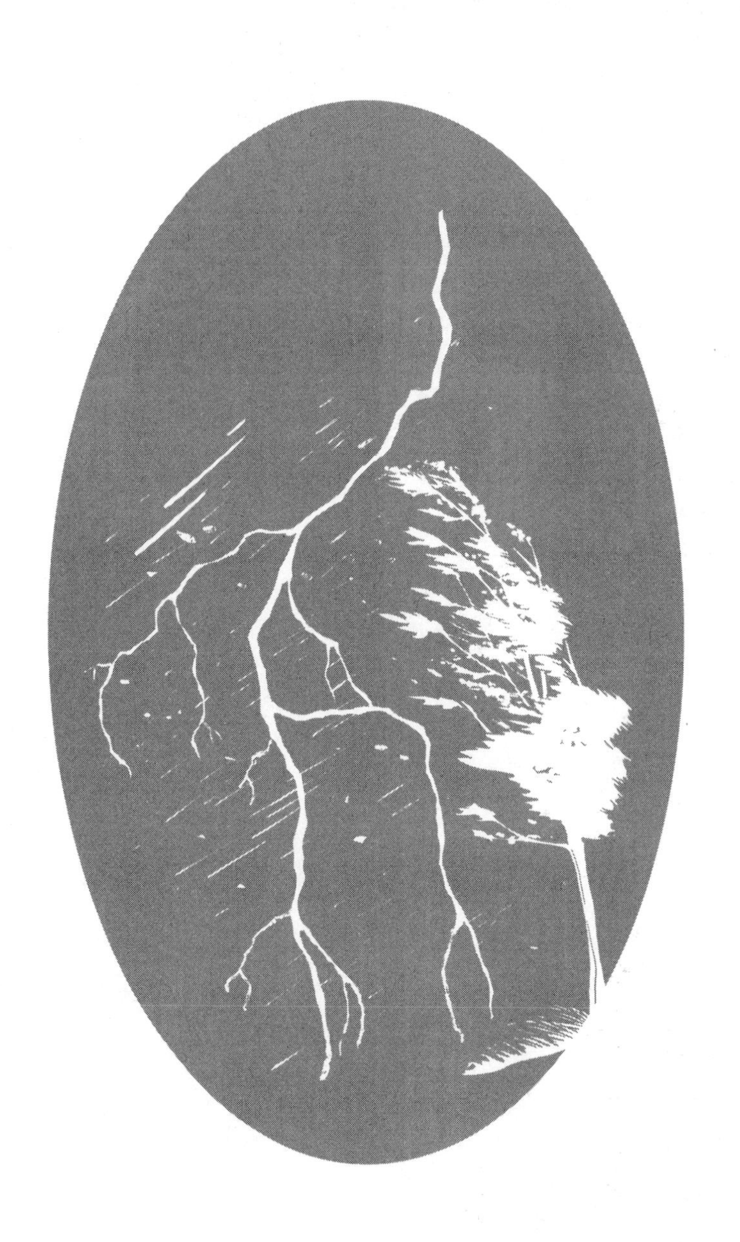

BONE

BOOM
KABABOOM

BONE. GET YOUR HEAD OVER BY THAT TREE AN' TAKE A LOOK AROUND.

GRAN'MA?

DO YOU THINK THE RAT CREATURES SAW US? MAYBE THEY DON'T KNOW WE'RE HERE.

THEY KNOW.
AN' IT WON'T BE LONG BEFORE THEY **FIND** US, EITHER.

I WISH YOU TWO HADN'T FOLLOWED ME OUT HERE.
WE WERE WORRIED ABOUT **YOU**!
WE WERE WORRIED YOU MIGHT DO SOME-THING **CRAZY**! LIKE RUN OUT HERE AN' PICK A **FIGHT** WITH TH' **DRAGON**!

THAT'S ENOUGH!
WHY ARE YOU SO **MAD** AT HIM?

I DON'T WANNA HEAR ANOTHER **WORD** OUT OF **YOU**, BONE! THIS WHOLE THING IS **YOUR** FAULT!

GRAN'MA! THAT'S NOT **TRUE!**
KEEP STILL, THORN! EVERYTHING WAS UNDER CONTROL UNTIL **HE** CAME TO OUR VALLEY AND **WOKE THE DRAGON!**

YOU KNOW MORE ABOUT THE DRAGON THAN **HE** DOES!
WHAT **I** KNOW ABOUT TH' DRAGON IS **MY** --

HOLD IT.

GET DOWN.
GET DOWN GET DOWN

RAT CREATURES.
I CAN'T TELL HOW CLOSE.

IT'S JUST ONE . . .
MUST BE A SCOUT.
HE'S COMING THIS WAY, BUT FROM TH' NOISE HE'S MAKIN', I DON'T THINK HE KNOWS WE'RE HERE, YET.

I'M GOIN' OUT THERE.
I WANT YOU TO SIT HERE AND NOT MOVE A MUSCLE! DO YOU UNDERSTAND ME?

DO YOU?!
YES.
UH, HUH.

OH, MAN.
THIS IS NOT GOOD.

I DON'T UNDERSTAND WHY SHE'S ACTING LIKE THIS, FONE BONE! SHE'S OUT OF CONTROL!

I WISH THE DRAGON WAS HERE.
WHOA.
DID YOU HEAR THAT?!

WHAT? I CAN'T HEAR ANYTHING EXCEPT THE RAIN - -

KRACK
BOOM

-- AND THE THUNDER!
WHAT DID YOU HEAR?
IT CAME FROM WHERE GRAN'MA BEN WENT!

IT --
SOUNDED LIKE A SCREAM!

OHH
...OR A SQUEAK!

MAYBE I IMAGINED IT.

WHAT SHOULD WE DO?
GRAN'MA BEN TOLD US NOT TO MOVE.

YOU'RE JUST GOING TO STARE AT THE PLACE WHERE SHE DISAPPEARED?
YES.

I KEEP THINKING I SEE SOMETHING; THEN IT'S NOTHING.

GRAN'MA --
STAY DOWN!

IT'S BAD.
TH' FOREST IS **SWARMING** WITH RAT CREATURES. AND THEY'RE MOVIN' **THIS WAY!**

WE CAN'T STAY **HERE** AND WE CAN'T GET BACK TO TH' **HOUSE** . . .

WE'RE GONNA HAFTA **OUTRUN 'EM.**

GRAN'MA, WHAT HAPPENED WITH TH' RAT CREATURE SCOUT? I THOUGHT I HEARD A SCREAM!
I TOOK CARE OF HIM. WITH ANY LUCK, WE'LL BE GONE BEFORE THEY FIND TH' BODY!

THE BODY?
YOU KILLED HIM?

WHERE DO YOU THINK YOU ARE? SAFE AT HOME IN BONEVILLE? IT'S ABOUT TIME YOU REALIZED THIS ISN'T A GAME, BONE!

LET'S GO.

SHE DIDN'T MEAN ANYTHING. SHE'S SCARED, TOO.
C'MON.
I NEVER THOUGHT IT WAS A GAME.

OHMYGOSH.
THORN! THEY SEE US!

HEY! LOOK OUT!!

SPLAT!

OHMYGOSH OHMYGOSH
HANG ON!

DRAGON! HELP US!

DRA-- MMMMF!

KEERAAKOW!

SNAP CRUNCH

KRACK!

THE DRAGON!
IT'S THE DRAGON!

HE CAME!
AN' HE CHASED OFF TH' RAT CREATURES!
WE'RE SAFE NOW!!

GET BEHIND TH' TREE.

KRACK KABOOM!

GRAN'MA! THE DRAGON JUST SAVED OUR LIVES! LEAVE HIM ALONE!

GRAN'MA?

PLEASE?

SIGH

KRAAAKKLE

I'M SO TIRED, BONE.

THANK YOU, GRAN'MA.

YOU THINK TH' DRAGON'LL BE THERE WHENEVER YOU NEED HIM . . .

. . . WELL, HE WON'T BE.

HE WASN'T ALWAYS THERE FOR ME.

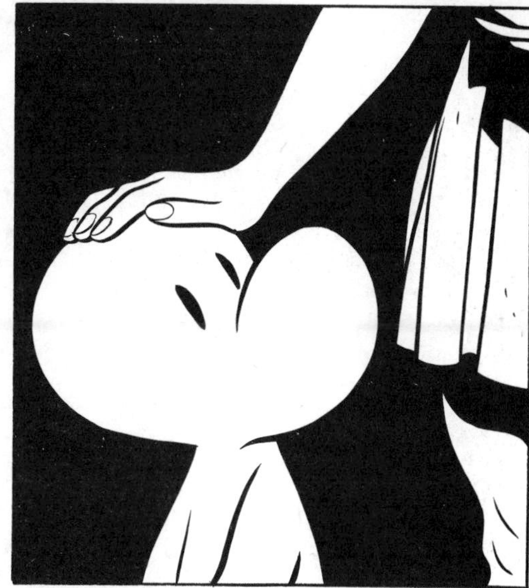

NEXT: GRAN'MA'S STORY

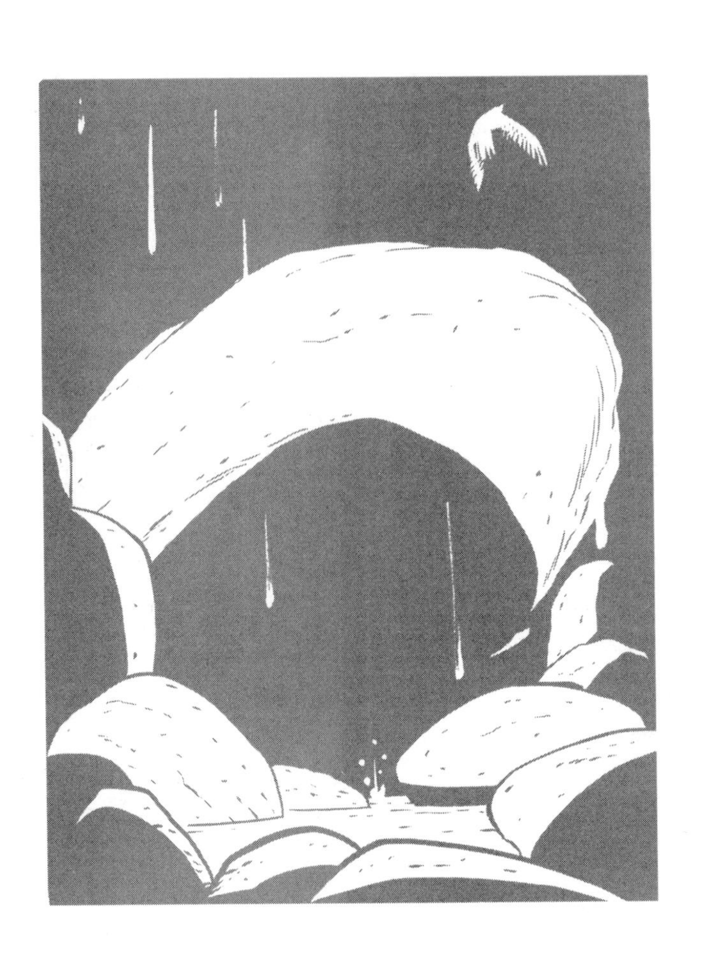

BONE
TM
WHAT ARE THEY SAYING?
I CAN NOT HEAR THEM . . .
shh!

GRAN'MA BEN?
CAN WE TALK TO YOU?

TALK AWAY.
I CAN LISTEN AN' MEND FENCES AT TH' SAME TIME.

AREN'T THOSE FENCES KINDA SMALL FOR KEEPIN' OUT RAT CREATURES?
THESE ARE COW FENCES, BONE. BUT I'M FIXIN' 'EM TO LET THE MONSTERS KNOW WHERE TH' BOUNDRIES ARE!
CHUNK

GRAN'MA - -
JUST A MOMENT, THORN. THERE'S SOMETHIN' I HAVE TO SAY TO FONE BONE . . .

YOU SAVED OUR LIVES DURING THAT STORM YESTERDAY. IF YOU HADN'T CALLED OUT FOR TH' DRAGON TO COME AN' CHASE OFF THE RAT CREATURES, WE MIGHT NOT'VE MADE IT. AND, WELL . . . THIS ISN'T EASY FOR ME, BUT . . . I OWE YOU AN APOLOGY FOR TH' WAY I BEEN TREATIN' YOU.
!

OH, NO, GRAN'MA. YOU DON'T OWE ME ANYTHING . . .
YES, I **DO.** EVER SINCE YOU **CAME** TO OUR VALLEY, I'VE BEEN **SUSPICIOUS** OF YOU AN' YOUR COUSINS . . .

I'VE **BLAMED** YOU BOYS FOR ALL THE RAT CREATURE ATTACKS AN' EVERYTHING **ELSE** THAT'S GONE WRONG . . .

. . . AN' IN PARTICULAR, I BLAMED **YOU** FOR DISTURBING TH' **DRAGON.**

TRUTH **IS,** OUR TROUBLES HERE IN TH' **VALLEY** STARTED A LONG TIME BEFORE **YOU** GOT HERE.

APOLOGY ACCEPTED, GRAN'MA.

GRAN'MA . . . FONE BONE HAS SOMETHING IN HIS **KNAPSACK** THAT I WANT HIM TO SHOW YOU.

WE THINK YOU BETTER TAKE A LOOK AT THIS.

WHAT TH' HECK IS IT?
JUST READ IT.
UM . . . FONE BONE, THIS ISN'T THE - -

My heart beats for you, my pookie so true... I love you so MUCHer and MUCHess...

GIVE ME THAT!
....so say you'll be mine, my sweet Valentine! from the Duke of Pook to the Duchess.
YOU WANTED ME TO READ A LOVE POEM?

THAT'S NOT TH' RIGHT THING! HERE! HERE! THIS IS IT! IT'S A MAP!

JEEZ!

THIS IS A **MAP?!** IT'S SO **FADED** I CAN'T MAKE **HEADS OR TAILS** OUTTA THIS THING!

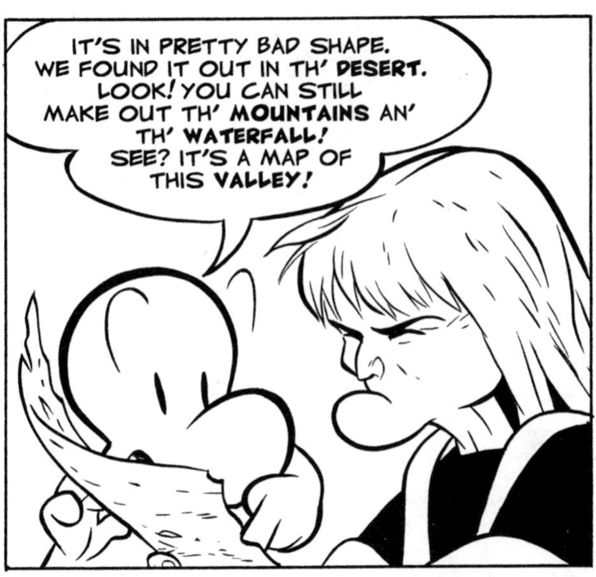
IT'S IN PRETTY BAD SHAPE. WE FOUND IT OUT IN TH' **DESERT.** LOOK! YOU CAN STILL MAKE OUT TH' **MOUNTAINS** AN' TH' **WATERFALL!** SEE? IT'S A MAP OF THIS **VALLEY!**

LOOKS LIKE IT WAS DRAWN BY A **FIVE-YEAR-OLD!**

IT WAS . . .

I DREW THAT MAP WHEN I WAS IN **DEREN GARD** WITH THE **DRAGONS.**

DON'T SAY ANOTHER WORD! THE FOREST HAS **EARS!**

INSIDE.
QUICKLY.

WELL?

WHERE DID YOU SAY YOU FOUND THAT **MAP?**
MY COUSINS AN' I FOUND IT AFTER WE GOT RUN OUTTA **BONEVILLE!**

WE WERE **LOST** OUT IN TH' **DESERT** AN' **SMILEY BONE** FOUND IT RIGHT BEFORE TH' **LOCUSTS** CAME AN' **SEPARATED** US!

LOCUSTS.
YES, MA'M.

WELL, NOW...
LOCUSTS. THAT'S --
-- NOT --

IT CAN'T MEAN **THAT** ANYMORE...
WHAT? **WHAT** CAN'T IT MEAN?!
GRAN'MA! IT'S TIME TO TELL US **THE TRUTH!**

FONE BONE . . .
BE A DEAR - -
RUN AND FETCH ME A DRINK OF WATER . . .
YES, M'AM.

GRANDMOTHER, I'M WAITING.

YES.
YES, OF COURSE YOU ARE . . .

. . . IT'S JUST SO DIFFICULT TO KNOW WHERE TO START.

WHY DON'T WE **START** WITH THE **DREAMS** I'VE HAD ALL MY LIFE ABOUT GROWING UP IN A **CAVE SURROUNDED BY DRAGONS?**
DREAMS THAT **YOU** TOLD ME NOT TO FEAR BECAUSE DRAGONS AREN'T **REAL!**

the dragon's stair
Defen gard

AFTER YOUR PARENTS DIED, IT FELL ON **ME** TO LOOK AFTER YOU . . .
AND . . .

. . . TO **HIDE** YOU.

THAT'S WHY, WHEN YOU WERE A LITTLE GIRL, I TOOK YOU TO LIVE WITH THE DRAGONS.
WHY?
WHY DID YOU **DO** IT, GRAN'MA?

FOR YOUR SAFETY, CHILD.
WHY DID YOU LIE TO ME?!
WHY DID YOU TELL ME THAT IT NEVER **HAPPENED?!** THAT **DRAGONS** DON'T EVEN **EXIST?!!**

I WAS TRYING TO PROTECT YOU.
I WAS TRYING TO PROTECT THE **WHOLE VALLEY.**
I CAN'T BELIEVE THIS.

I HAD A LOT OF **RESPONSIBILITIES** IN THOSE DAYS.

YOU NEEDED TO BE **HIDDEN** SO IT WOULDN'T START ALL OVER AGAIN.
HIDDEN? WHAT ARE YOU **TALKING** ABOUT?

WAR.
I'M TALKING ABOUT **WAR.**

THIS VALLEY HAS BEEN ON THE BRINK FOR **YEARS**, BONE. AND THAT'S SOMETHING THAT MUST NEVER, **EVER** HAPPEN AGAIN!

REMEMBER -- I FOUGHT THE RATS BACK IN THE **BIG WAR!**
BY THE TIME **SHE** WAS BORN, WE'D BEEN AT WAR WITH THE RATS CREATURES MOST OF MY **LIFE.**

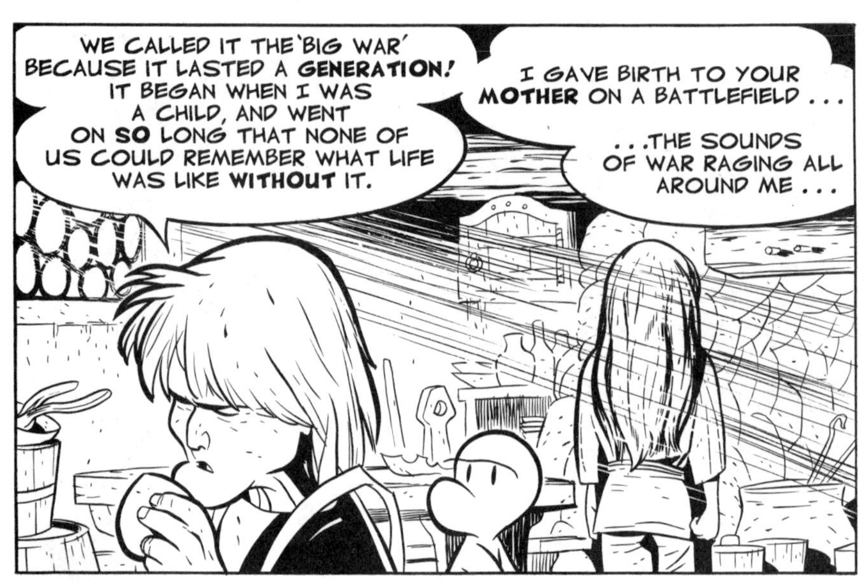

WE CALLED IT THE 'BIG WAR' BECAUSE IT LASTED A GENERATION! IT BEGAN WHEN I WAS A CHILD, AND WENT ON SO LONG THAT NONE OF US COULD REMEMBER WHAT LIFE WAS LIKE WITHOUT IT.
I GAVE BIRTH TO YOUR MOTHER ON A BATTLEFIELD . . .
. . .THE SOUNDS OF WAR RAGING ALL AROUND ME . . .

BUT THEN ONE DAY IT STOPPED. THE RAT CREATURES VANISHED, AND THE FIGHTING WAS OVER!

THERE WAS NO TREATY. THERE WAS NO SURRENDER. THE RAT CREATURES JUST DISAPPEARED WITHOUT A TRACE!

MOST OF THE PEOPLE OF THE VALLEY REJOICED, BUT I REMAINED SUSPICIOUS! I BELIEVED THE PULL-OUT WAS A PLOY - - A TRICK TO CATCH US OFF GUARD!
EVEN SO, ENOUGH TIME WENT BY THAT YOUR MOTHER GREW INTO A FINE, YOUNG WOMAN.

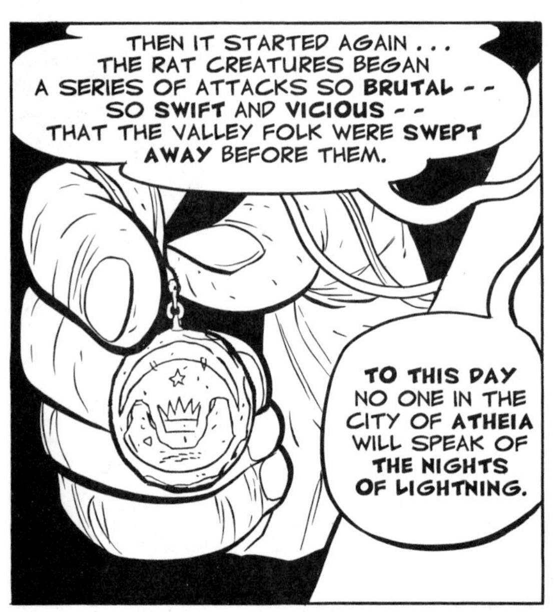

THEN IT STARTED AGAIN . . . THE RAT CREATURES BEGAN A SERIES OF ATTACKS SO BRUTAL - - SO SWIFT AND VICIOUS - - THAT THE VALLEY FOLK WERE SWEPT AWAY BEFORE THEM.
TO THIS DAY NO ONE IN THE CITY OF ATHEIA WILL SPEAK OF THE NIGHTS OF LIGHTNING.

I WAS AWAY UP HERE IN THE NORTH, AS I OFTEN WAS IN THOSE DAYS, PREPARING AN ALLIANCE BETWEEN DRAGONS AND MEN, WHEN I RECEIVED WORD THAT THE CASTLE HAD BEEN TAKEN! ATHEIA HAD FALLEN.
GRAN'MA BEN . . . WHY DID THORN NEED TO BE HIDDEN?

THIS IS DIFFICULT ENOUGH, BONE, WITHOUT YOU PUSHING ME.
I'M SORRY, BUT IT HAS SOMETHING TO DO WITH THORN'S DREAMS, DOESN'T IT? ALL THE DREAMS ABOUT DRAGONS AND HOODED PEOPLE!

IN ONE OF MY DREAMS, GRAN'MA, I AM TAKEN OVER THE MOUNTAINS AT NIGHT BY PEOPLE WHOSE FACES I CAN NOT SEE . . .

. . . THEY HAVE HOODS PULLED DOWN TO HIDE THEMSELVES.
I THINK ONE OF THEM IS YOU.

THEN, SOMEWHERE HIGH IN THE MOUNTAINS, WE ARE BETRAYED!

THE OTHERS ARE ATTACKED BY RAT CREATURES, AND YOU ARE FORCED TO DELIVER ME INTO THE HANDS OF THE DRAGONS BY YOURSELF.

SIT DOWN.

YOUR MOTHER AND FATHER DID NOT DROWN WHEN YOU WERE AN INFANT.
THEY WERE THE RULING **MONARCHS** OF THE REALM.
AND THEY, ALONG WITH A NURSEMAID, MANAGED TO SNEAK YOU OUT OF ATHEIA.

GO ON.

TRAVELING ONLY AT NIGHT, AND IN COMPLETE SECRECY, THEY MANAGED TO MAKE THEIR WAY **NORTH** ALONG THE FOOTHILLS OF THE MOUNTAINS TO THE PASS CALLED **THE DRAGON'S STAIR.**

I MET THE ROYAL PARTY THERE ON THE PASS . . .
I WAS ESCOURTING THEM TO THE DRAGONS' STRONGHOLD IN **DEREN GARD** WHEN WE WERE **BETRAYED!**

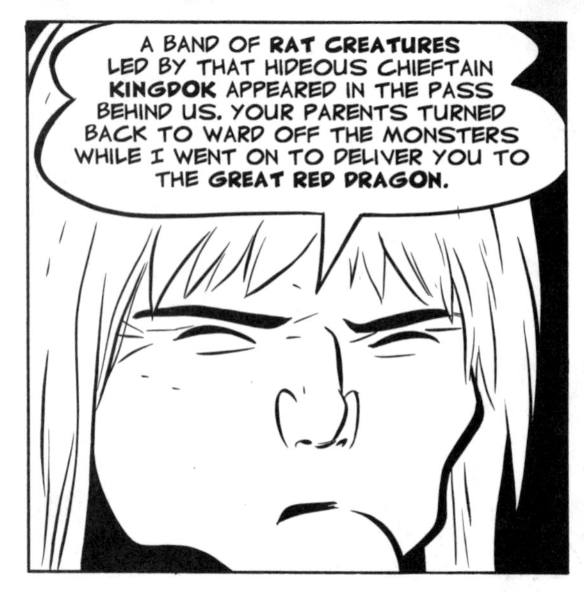
A BAND OF **RAT CREATURES** LED BY THAT HIDEOUS CHIEFTAIN **KINGDOK** APPEARED IN THE PASS BEHIND US. YOUR PARENTS TURNED BACK TO WARD OFF THE MONSTERS WHILE I WENT ON TO DELIVER YOU TO THE **GREAT RED DRAGON.**

IT WAS THE **NURSEMAID** WHO BETRAYED US.
SHE WAS **EAGER** TO RETURN TO THE MONSTERS. I DON'T KNOW WHAT SHE RECEIVED FOR HER **TREACHERY**, BUT SHE DIDN'T LIVE TO ENJOY IT.
WHEN I RETURNED TO THE SITE OF THE AMBUSH, THE **MASSACRE** WAS OVER.
THE TRAITOROUS MAID HAD BEEN TORN IN TWO.

THE KING WAS DEAD. AND YOUR MOTHER - - MY ONLY CHILD - - THE QUEEN LIE STILL IN THE STARLIGHT. THE FINAL VICTIMS OF THE NIGHTS OF LIGHTNING.

THAT'S WHEN TH' DRAGON FAILED YOU, ISN'T IT? HE COULDN'T BE THERE FOR YOU, BECAUSE HE WAS WITH THORN.
MY MOTHER AND FATHER . . .

WERE KING AND QUEEN OF ATHEIA. AND I WAS QUEEN OF THE LAND BEFORE THEM.
YOU, THORN HARVESTAR, ARE THE CROWN PRINCESS OF THE REALM AND YOU HAVE MANY ENEMIES.

MY GREATEST FEAR NOW, IS THAT YOUR ENEMIES MAY BE MORE POWERFUL THAN EVEN I EVER DREAMED.

IF ONE OF YOUR ENEMIES IS THE LORD OF THE LOCUSTS, THEN WAR IS UNAVOIDABLE . . .

. . . AND I HAVE FAILED.

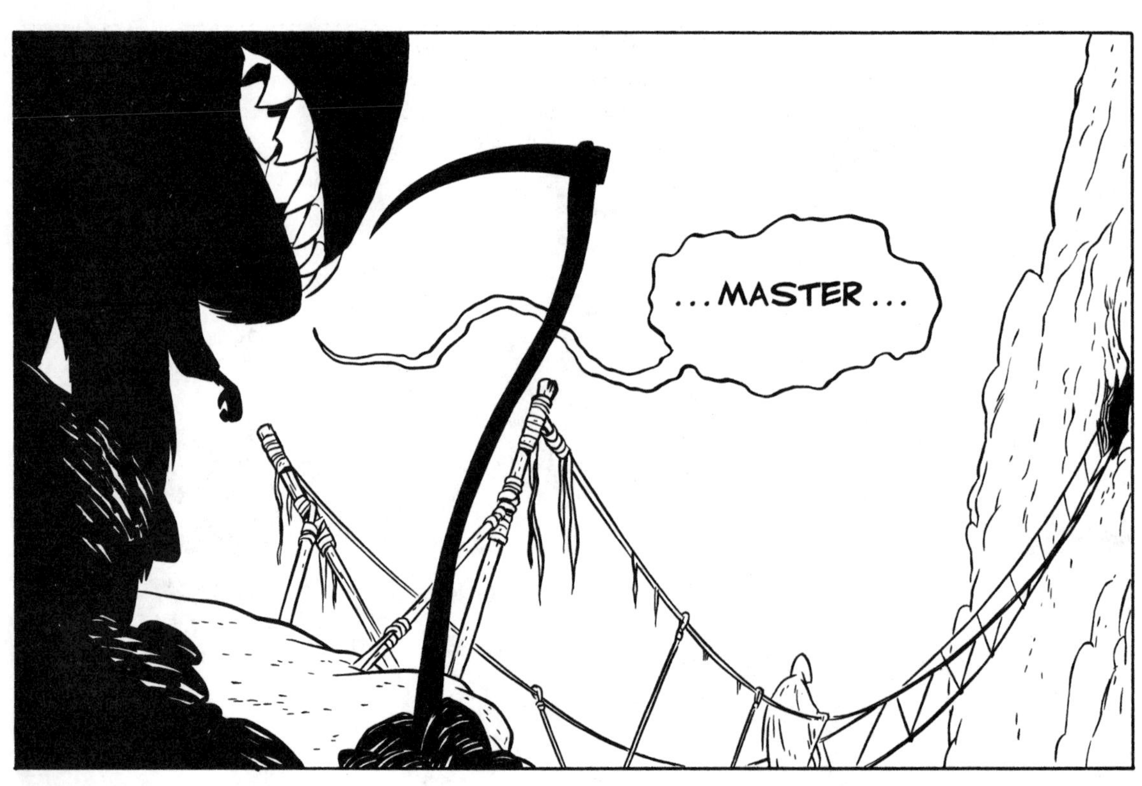
...MASTER...

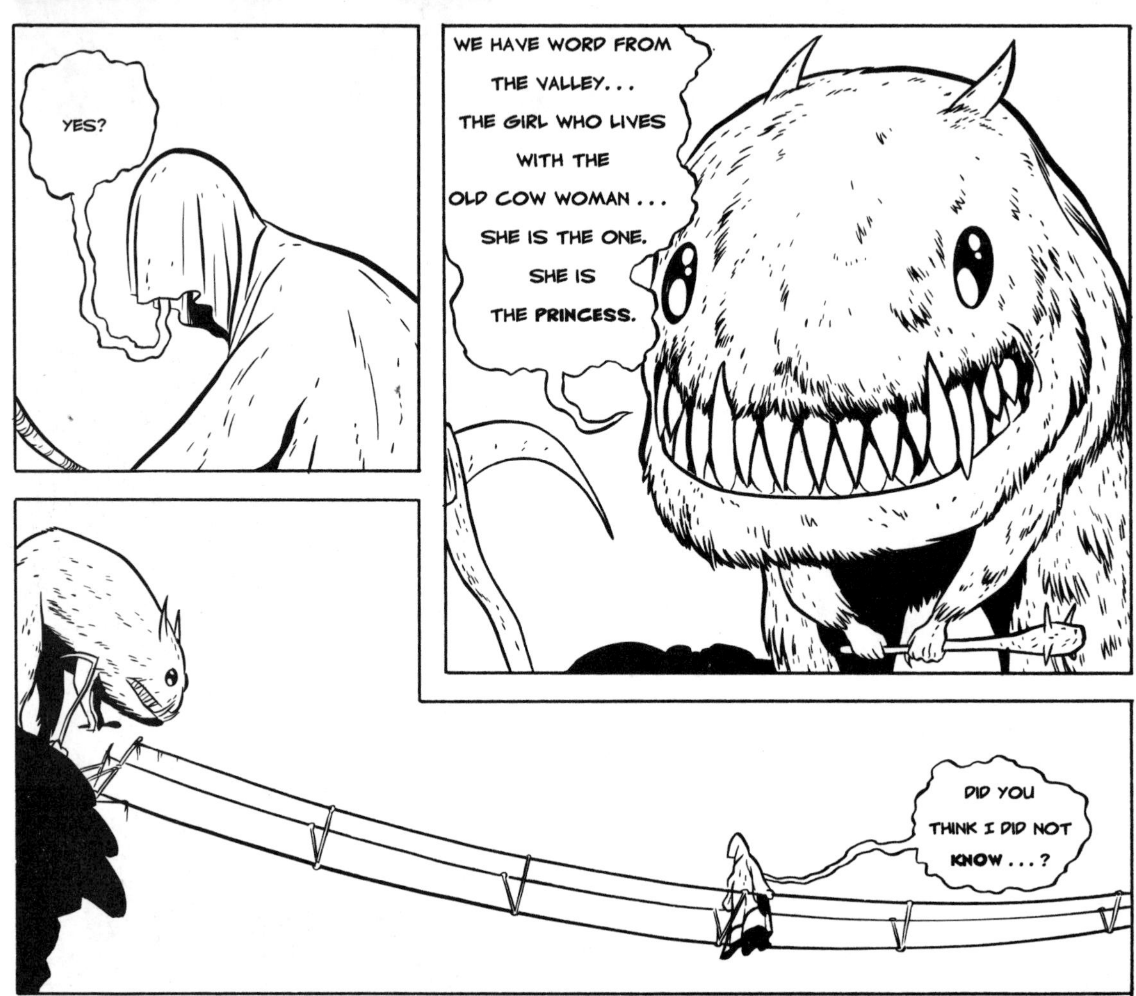
YES?
WE HAVE WORD FROM THE VALLEY... THE GIRL WHO LIVES WITH THE OLD COW WOMAN... SHE IS THE ONE. SHE IS THE PRINCESS.
DID YOU THINK I DID NOT KNOW...?

. . . MASTER?

. . . IF I WAITED . . .
FOR YOUR COWARDLY UNDERLINGS TO BRING ME INFORMATION . . . . . WE WOULD ALL GROW OLD LISTENING TO SILENCE . . . . .

I SUSPECT THAT IF **YOU**, KINGDOK . . . SHOWED LESS **FEAR** FOR THE RED DRAGON . . . YOUR WARRIORS MIGHT FOLLOW YOUR EXAMPLE . . .

NOW LEAVE ME . . .

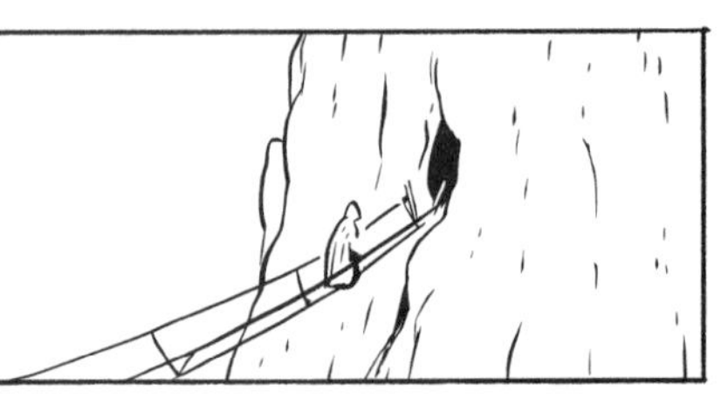

WHAT NEWS DO YOU BRING US?

WE HAVE OUR ARMY.
THE POPULATION OF THE CAMP IS NEARING FIVE HUNDRED THOUSAND . . . MORE RECRUITS ARRIVE EACH MORNING . . .
THAT IS GOOD.

THERE IS SOMETHING ELSE YOU WISH TO ASK US ABOUT?

THE GIRL . . . HER DREAMS ARE LIKE A BEACON . . . AND YET I CAN NOT **REACH** HER . . .
IS HER STRENGTH SO GREAT?

EVEN IN HER IGNORANCE, HER STRENGTH IS GREAT . . . BUT THERE IS SOMETHING MORE . . . AS I REACHED OUT TO HER . . . A **NEW** BEACON APPEARED . . .
THE RED DRAGON SEEKS TO BRING A PAWN INTO PLAY. DO NOT CONCERN YOURSELF.
WHAT NEWS DO YOU BRING US OF THE ONE WE SEEK?

THE ONE WHO BEARS A STAR IS AGAIN WITH THE VILLAGERS . . . IF IT IS YOUR DESIRE . . . WE WILL ATTACK THE TOWN.
AWAIT OUR INSTRUCTIONS.

MY LORD . . . THE RED DRAGON IS DANGEROUS. SHOULD WE NOT PREPARE - -
ASK NO MORE QUESTIONS.

NEXT: GRAN'MA'S STORY PART II

BONE
The Barrel-Haven
L. Down. Prop.
EVERYBODY GATHER 'ROUND! I GOT A LITTLE ANNOUNCEMENT TO MAKE!
THAT MEANS YOU, WENDELL!
AN' YOU TOO, EUCLID!
ALL RIGHT NOW, LISTEN UP! I'M GONNA TELL YA ABOUT A CONTEST!
BUT FIRST . . .

I KNOW HOW YOU FELLAS FEEL ABOUT THESE **BONE** BOYS . . .

. . . YOU WANNA **KILL** 'EM FOR MESSIN' WITH **TH' COW RACE!**

RRR!
GRR!
RRR!
GRR!
RRR!
RRRR!
WELL, **SO DO I**, BUT THEY OWE ME A **LOTTA** EGGS, AN' SO THEY GOTTA STAY **RIGHT HERE** AN' WORK IT OFF!

THAT MEANS I DON'T WANT **NO TROUBLE** FROM YOU GUYS. YOU GOT ME?
WHY NOT, LUCIUS? THEY GOTTA **PAY** FOR WHAT THEY DID!
I SAY WE TEAR THEIR LEGS OFF!

YEAH!
THEY TRIED TO MAKE **FOOLS** OUTTA US!
YOU MADE FOOLS OUTTA **YERSELVES!**

YOU LET THIS FAST-TALKIN' SQUIRT TRICK YA INTO BETTIN' ON A COW THAT DIDN'T EVEN EXIST!
ISN'T THAT WHAT HAPPENED, PHONEY BONE?
YEAH, YEAH. THAT'S IT. WE DON'T NEED TO DWELL ON IT.

YOU LET YERSELVES BE TALKED INTO BETTIN' YER LIFE'S SAVINGS ON THIS IDIOT DRESSED IN A COW SUIT!
IS IT ME, OR IS IT GETTING STUFFY IN HERE?

BUT I WARNED YA! I TOLD YA YOU WERE BEIN' PLAYED FOR A BUNCHA SAPS, BUT YA DIDN'T LISTEN TO ME, DID JA? HUH? DID JA?

THAT'S RIGHT! AN' WHEN GRAN'MA BEN WON THAT RACE, I WAS TH' ONLY ONE WHO BET ON HER! ME AN' GRAN'MA COULDA SPLIT THAT POT, BUT NOOOOO . . . .
WE FELT SORRY FOR YA!

ALL BETS WERE OFF, AN' WE LET YA HAVE YER LIVESTOCK BACK! ALL TOLD, I'D SAY YOU GIRLS GOT OFF PRETTY EASY!

GRR
RR
OKAY, NOW THAT **THAT'S** SETTLED, I WANNA TELL YA ABOUT THIS LITTLE **CONTEST** WE'RE GONNA HAVE . . .
RRR
. . . **THESE** TWO - -

KILL`EM!
RIP THEIR HEADS OFF!
!

BACK OFF OR I START SWINGIN'

HERE'S TH' DEAL, SEE? AS LONG AS PHONEY BONE AN' HIS COUSIN SMILEY BONE ARE **WORKIN'** HERE, NOBODY LAYS A **FINGER** ON 'EM OR THEY ANSWER TO **ME? CLEAR?!**

CLEAR.
ALL RIGHT THEN.

. . . NOW, THIS **CONTEST** I WAS TELLIN' YOU ABOUT - - IT'S BETWEEN **ME** AN' MISTER **PHONEY BONE**, HERE. HE THINKS HE CAN RUN THIS JOINT **BETTER** THAN **I** CAN! WE'RE GONNA LET **YOU** DECIDE!

FROM NOW ON, THIS BAR WILL BE DIVIDED IN **TWO! I'LL** RUN **THIS** END, AN' TH' **BONES**'LL RUN **THAT** END.

HERE'S TH' RULES: YOU CAN TAKE YER BUSINESS TO WHICHEVER END OF TH' BAR YOU **WANT!** AFTER **ONE** MOON, THE END THAT EARNS TH' **MOST EGGS** FOR TH' TAVERN **WINS!!**

YOU CAN EITHER VOTE FOR **ME**, OR YOU CAN VOTE FOR **PHONEY!**
EVERYBODY UNDERSTAND TH' RULES?
GOOD!

WHO WANTS A DRINK?

WHAT ARE WE GONNA DO, PHONEY? NOBODY'S GONNA ORDER ANYTHING FROM **US!** IF WE LOSE THIS CONTEST WE'RE GONNA BE WASHIIN' **DISHES** FOR TH' REST OF OUR **LIVES!**

I KNOW, I KNOW. THIS WASN'T ONE OF TH' **SMARTEST** BETS I'VE EVER MADE.
BUT WE'LL THINK OF **SOMETHIN'**, RIGHT? WE ALWAYS **DO!**

SURE! ALL WE GOTTA DO IS COME UP WITH SOME WAY TO **LURE** TH' TOWNSPEOPLE BACK DOWN TO **OUR** END. HOW HARD CAN **THAT** BE?
RIGHT! I'M **ON** IT! WE'LL HOLD A LECTURE SERIES! WE COULD TRY THOSE **DANCE ROUTINES** I'VE BEEN WORKIN' ON . . . NO - - WAIT! I'VE **GOT** IT! **PUPPETS!**

GROAN
WE'RE DEAD.

GRAN'MA BEN?

THORN --
. . . UM . . .
I MEAN, PRINCESS --
DON'T CALL ME THAT.

SORRY.

ALL THOSE DREAMS . . .
THEY WERE REAL.

THOSE DREAMS WERE MEMORIES OF THINGS THAT REALLY HAPPENED TO ME.

SOMETHING LIKE THAT.
THEY WERE JUST LIKE YOU SAID...

IN MY DREAMS I WAS TAKEN OUT OF A BURNING PALACE AS A LITTLE GIRL...

...AND IN THE DARK OF NIGHT, I WAS BROUGHT OVER THE MOUNTAINS TO THE DRAGONS' CAVE...

I EVEN DREAMED ABOUT THE AMBUSH ON THE DRAGON'S STAIR! I DREAMED ABOUT THE MURDER OF MY PARENTS AND I DIDN'T EVEN KNOW IT!
HOW CAN THIS BE?! HOW CAN I DREAM ABOUT THINGS THAT HAPPENED TO ME, BUT NOT REMEMBER THEM HAPPENING?!

SOMETIMES DREAMS KNOW MORE THAN WE DO.

WHAT HAPPENS IN YOUR DREAM AFTER YOU GET TO THE DRAGONS' CAVE?

TRY TO REMEMBER, THORN.
I . . . I'M BEING LED INTO THE CAVE. IT'S VERY DARK AT FIRST . . .

. . . BUT THEN MY EYES GET USED TO THE BLACKNESS . . . I'M AWARE OF **SHAPES** IN THE CAVE AROUND ME . . .

. . . I CAN SEE NOW . . . THERE IS **LIGHT** . . . I AM IN A HUGE CAVERN . . . SURROUNDED BY **DRAGONS**. **DOZENS** OF THEM. AND WE'RE ALL LOOKING AT SOMETHING . . .

WHAT? WHAT ARE YOU LOOKING AT?
IT'S WHERE THE LIGHT IS COMING FROM. I... I THINK IT **MIGHT** BE A **THRONE**...

WHO'S **ON** TH' THRONE?
AH... I CAN'T SEE THAT. THERE MIGHT NOT BE **ANYBODY** ON THE THRONE.

WHAT ELSE?
AFTER THAT I STAYED WITH THE DRAGONS. BUT I NEVER SAW THAT CHAMBER AGAIN... **OR** THE THRONE.

WHAT ABOUT THE **GARDEN?** DON'T YOU WANT TO TELL GRAN'MA BEN ABOUT **THAT?**

SHE HEARD IT. SHE WAS **LISTENING IN** ON OUR CONVERSATION OUT IN THE **BARN.**

YES, I HEARD YOU. YOU WERE TALKING ABOUT **DRAGONS** AND **DREAMS.**

...BUT I WASN'T **EAVES-DROPPING.** I JUST CAME IN FROM THE RAIN.

GRAN'MA, THORN'S DREAM WAS ABOUT A DARK, SHADOWY FIGURE WHO WORE A **HOOD** PULLED DOWN OVER HIS FACE. WAS HE **GOOD**, OR WAS HE THE **LORD OF THE LOCUSTS**?

I DON'T KNOW.
I DON'T KNOW WHAT TO **THINK** ANYMORE . . .

I THOUGHT THE **LORD OF THE LOCUSTS** WAS DEAD - -
- - **KILLED** A LONG TIME AGO WHEN I WAS VERY, VERY YOUNG . . . **BEFORE** THE WAR.

BUT YOU'RE **SURE** THE DRAGON WAS IN **YOUR** DREAM, RIGHT?
I **GUESS** SO, BUT I STILL DON'T UNDERSTAND - -

MMMM.
HE GAVE ME HIS **WORD** . . .
WHAT?
WHAT DID HE GIVE YOU HIS WORD ON?
- - THAT HE WOULDN'T BE IN MY **DREAM**? I DON'T **GET** IT!

C'MON, GRAN'MA! I HAVE A RIGHT TO KNOW! HOW AM I MIXED UP IN THIS? DOES IT HAVE SOMETHING TO DO WITH MY COUSINS?

THORN?

SLAM!

THORN!

HEY!

WAIT UP.

YOU FEEL OKAY?
I DON'T FEEL **ANYTHING.**

DO YOU WANT ME TO LEAVE YOU ALONE?

OKAY. I'LL GO.

I'M SORRY.
LISTEN. IF YOU NEED **ANYTHING**, JUST . . . UH . . . JUST **TELL** ME, ALL RIGHT?

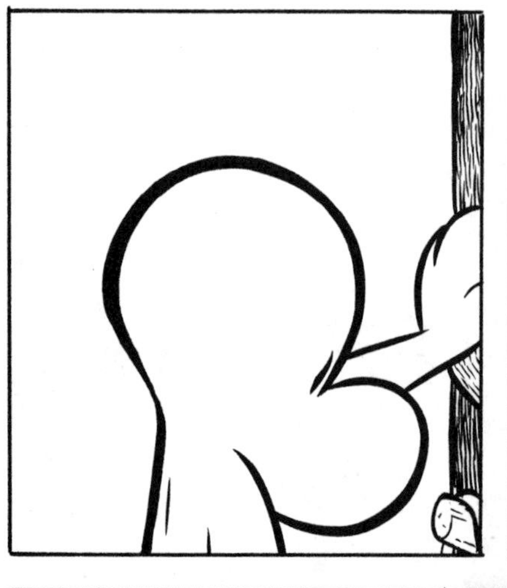

HEY, EVERYBODY! COME OVER HERE AN' TRY SOME BEER!

RRRR.
I KNEW PUPPETS WOULDN'T WORK.

WELL, THAT'S IT! WE'RE BEATEN! NOBODY WANTS ANYTHING FROM US! READY TO THROW IN TH' TOWEL, CUZ?

ARE YOU CRAZY? THAT GORILLA CAN'T BEAT ME! ESPECIALLY WHEN IT COMES TO TURNIN' A PROFIT!

YOU KEEP TRYIN' TO THINK OF SOMETHIN'! I'M GONNA GO DOWN AN' TAKE A LOOK AT WHAT HE'S DOIN'.
I'M PUTTIN' ON MY THINKIN' CAP!

WELL, WELL, WELL, WELL . . . LOOK WHAT SLITHERED UP! READY TO CALL IT QUITS, SMART-GUY?
I ADMIT THIS MIGHT BE A LITTLE TOUGHER THAN I THOUGHT.

YOU'RE WELCOME TO HANG AROUND THIS END. YOU MIGHT LEARN SOMETHIN' ABOUT RUNNIN' A BUSINESS HERE ON TH' WINNING END OF TH' BAR!
DON'T GET SMUG! IT AIN'T OVER YET!
HEY -- WHAT'S EVERYBODY DOIN'?

HUH? HEY!
HEY!
WHERE'S EVERYBODY GOIN'?

WHAT TH'? WHAT'S GOIN' ON?
HOLY COW!

LOOKS LIKE TH' TABLES HAVE BEEN TURNED, PAL! EXCUSE ME WHILE I GET BACK TO TH' WINNING END OF TH' BAR!

MAN!
WHADDYA DOIN', SMILEY? GIVIN' THIS STUFF AWAY?

GIMME THAT!
GIMME THAT!
HERE! HERE! YOU! GIMME THAT!
EVERYBODY! HAND 'EM OVER!

WHAT, ARE YOU CRAZY?! HOW ARE WE SUPPOSED TO TURN A PROFIT IF YOU GIVE TH' BEER AWAY?!!
I'VE HAD IT WITH THAT RUNT.
ME, TOO.
LUCIUS OR NO LUCIUS, THIS TIME LET'S FIX 'EM FOR GOOD!

GET 'EM!

NEXT: PHONEY the DRAGONSLAYER

BONE™
GO ON, BONE! ANSWER HIM!
YEAH, ANSWER ME!
WHAT DID YOU SAY ABOUT A DRAGON?
GULP!

I - - I - - UH - -
I JUST SAID I WISH FONE BONE'S **DRAGON** WAS HERE . . .

GASP!
GASP!
FONE BONE HAS A DRAGON?
GASP!
I DON'T BELIEVE IT.

WHO'S **FONE BONE?**
HE'S THAT **OTHER** BONE! THEIR **COUSIN!**

YEAH, RIGHT . . .
TH' ONE WHO'S ALWAYS HANGIN' AROUND WITH **THORN!**

SO WHERE IS THIS COUSIN OF YOURS **NOW?**
YEAH! AN' WHERE'S THE DRAGON?!
ALL RIGHT, **THAT'S** ENOUGH!
QUIT CROWDIN' TH' **BAR!**

DON'T TRY TO STOP US, LUCIUS! IF THERE'S A DRAGON WALKIN' AROUND OUT THERE, WE WANNA KNOW!
WHAT FOR? YOU DON'T BELIEVE IN DRAGONS, DO YOU?

I DIDN'T SAY I BELIEVED IN 'EM . . . BUT THERE HAVE BEEN SOME PRETTY STRANGE THINGS GOIN' ON HERE LATELY!
STRANGE ENOUGH TO MAKE YOU START BELIEVIN' IN CHILDREN'S STORIES?

I KNOW IT SOUNDS CRAZY, BUT PEOPLE BEEN SEEIN' STRANGE THINGS IN TH' WOODS AT NIGHT! FOLKS ARE AFRAID TO GO OUT!
IT'S TRUE!

AN' TH' HAIRY MEN! THEY'RE SURE GETTIN' A LOT BRAVER! YOU NEVER USED TO SEE THEM AROUND . . . AN' NOW YOU HEAR STORIES ABOUT 'EM EVERY DAY!
YEAH! THEY EVEN ATTACKED TH' COW RACE IN BROAD DAYLIGHT!
I WAS THERE, REMEMBER? WHAT'S YOUR POINT?

IT ALL STARTED JUST ABOUT TH' SAME TIME THESE TWO SHOWED UP!
EVERYTHING WAS FINE UNTIL TH' THE BONES CAME TO OUR PART OF TH' VALLEY!

NOW ALL WE GOT IS TROUBLE!
LOOK HERE, BUB, I DON'T KNOW WHOSE DRAGON THIS IS, BUT IT AIN'T OURS! TH' ONLY DRAGON I'VE SEEN IS A BIG, LAZY ORANGE ONE, AN' HE WAS ALREADY HERE!

GASP!
I GOT NEWS FOR YA, GASPING-BOY! YOU GOT A LOTTA WEIRD STUFF IN THIS CRAZY VALLEY, SO DON'T GO BLAMIN' US FOR YOUR DRAGON PROBLEMS!

BIG AN' ORANGE! THEN IT'S TRUE!
WHAT'S TRUE? YOU'RE NOT GONNA BELIEVE ANYTHING PHONEY BONE TELLS YOU, ARE YA? YOU CAN'T TRUST THIS RUNT AS FAR AS YOU CAN THROW HIM!

HE'S TELLIN' TH' TRUTH, LUCIUS! WE GOT US A REAL, LIVE DRAGON WALKIN' AROUND OUT THERE!
YOU TAKE TH' CAKE, WENDELL, YOU KNOW THAT?

JONATHAN! TELL LUCIUS WHAT YOU TOLD US!
UM . . . ONE NIGHT WHEN I WAS WALKIN' HOME . . . UH . . . I SAW SOMETHIN'. . .
SPIT IT OUT, BOY.

THERE WASN'T HARDLY ANY MOON OUT, SO IT WAS KINDA DARK. AN' REAL QUIET. THEN I SAW IT. A HUGE, SHAPE MOVIN' BETWEEN TH' TREES! IT WAS BIG AND IT WAS ORANGE - - AND WHEN IT WAS GONE, ALL THAT WAS LEFT WAS TH' SMELL OF BRIMSTONE!

THERE, SEE? WHAT DO YOU SAY TO THAT, LUCIUS? STILL THINK DRAGONS ARE JUST CHILDREN'S STORIES?
AAH! I AIN'T GOT NOTHIN' TO SAY. . .

WELL, WELL! NOW, THIS IS INTERESTING . . .

YOU SAY YOU'VE SEEN SHAPES IN TH' WOODS . . . HEARD BUMPS IN TH' NIGHT . . .

. . . YOU SAY IT'S NOT SAFE TO GO OUTSIDE AFTER DARK . . .

YESSIR, I'VE SEEN THESE SYMPTOMS BEFORE!

OH, YOU THINK IT'LL NEVER HAPPEN IN A NICE, QUIET, LITTLE TOWN LIKE THIS. . . BUT YOU CAN'T STOP 'EM! THEY'RE HERE TO STAY!

WHAT ARE YOU TALKIN' ABOUT?
WELL, I HATE TO SAY THIS, BUT I THINK IT'S SAFE TO ASSUME THAT IF YOU HAVE ONE DRAGON, THERE'S BOUND TO BE OTHERS!

OH, MY GOSH! THERE'S PROBABLY DRAGONS EVERYWHERE!
I KNEW IT! THEY'RE TRYIN' TO TAKE OVER!

WHO KNOWS? THIS COULD BE A MAJOR INFESTATION!
NOW, YOU CAN EITHER IGNORE THIS PROBLEM, OR YOU CAN DO SOMETHIN' ABOUT IT!

HE'S RIGHT! WE GOTTA DO SOMETHIN' BEFORE IT'S TOO LATE!
RRR!
IT'S US AGAINST THEM!
WE'RE NOT GONNA TAKE THIS SITTIN' DOWN!

TELL US WHAT WE GOTTA DO!
THE SAME THING YOU DO WHEN YOU GOT ANY KIND OF PEST CONTROL PROBLEM . . . YOU GET AN EXTERMINATOR!
RRR!

AND WHERE DO WE GET AN EXTERMINATOR?
YER LOOKIN' AT ONE!
PHONCIBLE P. BONE: DRAGONSLAYER!
AT YOUR SERVICE!
GRRR!
RRR!

WHAT TH' HELL DO YOU THINK YOU'RE DOIN'?
YOU KNOW THIS LITTLE BET YOU AN' I GOT GOIN' TO SEE WHO CAN SELL TH' MOST BEER?

YEAH?
I'M ABOUT TO WIN!

SMILEY! START POURIN'!
NOTHIN' LIKE A LITTLE ALCOHOL TO GREASE TH' WHEELS OF MOB MENTALITY! RIGHT, BOYS?!

RIGHT!
YAY!
THE FIRST ROUND'S ON ME! BUT AFTER THAT, YOU GOTTA PAY!

THREE CHEERS FOR PHONEY!
THAT'S IT!

THIS HAS GONE **FAR ENOUGH!** I----

WELCOME, STRANGER. CAN I HELP YOU? YOU NEED A ROOM, OR JUST LOOKIN' TO SLAKE YOUR THIRST?

I BRING NEWS FROM THE SOUTH.
WAIT FOR ME OUTSIDE.

HEY, THERE, FONE BONE! HOW YOU DOIN' THESE FINE DAYS?

HELLO, TED! I'M DOIN' OKAY . . . THORN AN' GRAN'MA BEN COULD BE BETTER . . .
HOW ABOUT YOU?
GOOD! JUST BEEN TA SEE LUCIUS AN' YER COUSINS!

OH, YEAH? HOW ARE THEY? ARE THEY CAUSIN' ANY TROUBLE?
THEY'S KICKIN' UP SOME DUST, YOU KNOW, JES LIKE THEY DO. BUT WHAT'S ALL THIS YOU SAYIN' 'BOUTS GRAN'MA AN' THORNY? SOMETHIN' WRONG?

WELL, THORN IS OUT IN TH' BARN LAYIN' FACE DOWN IN TH' HAY. SHE'S PRETTY UPSET. SHE GOT SOME BAD NEWS ABOUT HER PARENTS, AN' SOME OTHER STUFF ABOUT HER PAST . . .
LIKE WHAT?

OH, UH, I PROBABLY SHOULDN'T SAY, TED. I MEAN, I TRUST YOU, BUT I THINK THEY'RE KINDA SECRET - -
SHE FIND OUT HER FOLKS WAS KILLED BY RAT CREATURES?

OBOY. GRAN'MA TOLD HER, HUH? SO I SUPPOSE SHE KNOWS HER REAL LAST NAME IS HARVESTAR . . . THA'S A ROYAL NAME, Y'KNOW.

UM, YEAH. SHE KNOWS. GRAN'MA TOLD HER.
THORN HARVESTAR. CROWN PRINCESS OF TH' WHOLE SHOOTIN' MATCH! BIG STUFF, BIG STUFF.

HOW DID YOU KNOW THAT? THORN DIDN'T EVEN KNOW!
BUGS KNOW A LOTTA STUFF FOLKS WOULDN'T S'POSE THEY'D KNOW.
SAY, THAT REMINDS ME, I GOT A IMPORTANT MESSAGE FROM LUCIUS FOR GRAN'MA BEN! WHERE IS SHE?

SHE WAS IN TH' HOUSE LAST I SAW HER.
OKEE DOKEE, BONE! CATCH YA LATER, BYE!

BYE!

SLAM!

HEY, BONE! GO GRAB YOUR KNAPSACK AN' MEET ME IN TH' BARN! NOW!

YES, MA'M!

SHUNK

GET UP, THORN.
I JUST RECEIVED WORD THAT TH' SITUATION DOWN SOUTH HAS CHANGED ...

GRAN'MA - - ?
WE HAVE TO LEAVE.

HERE'S YOUR BEDROLL AND A FEW OF YOUR PERSONAL THINGS . . .

C'MON IN HERE, BONE.
THE DEFENSES IN ATHEIA HAVE BEEN LAX FOR SOME TIME, BUT APPARENTLY THERE'S BEEN A BREACH . . .

MASSIVE TROOP MOVEMENTS HAVE BEEN SEEN ALONG THE EASTERN MOUNTAIN RANGE NORTH OF THE OLD ABANDONED BORDER CROSSING IN SOUTHERN PAWA.

IT SEEMS LARGE NUMBERS OF RAT CREATURES ARE HEADING THIS WAY.

HERE? THEY'RE COMING HERE? WHY?
THEY'RE NOT OUT ON A PICNIC, BONE! IT'S NOT SAFE HERE ANYMORE. WE HAVE TO LEAVE NOW. ANYTHING IN TH' HOUSE YOU NEED BEFORE WE GET STARTED?

I -- MIGHT NEED SOMETHING WARMER TO WEAR . . .

I'LL GRAB YOUR CLOAK WHEN I GO BACK IN FOR TH' FOOD. AND WHILE I'M DOIN' THAT I WANT YOU TO CLEAR AWAY ALL THIS STRAW.

THERE'S A SECRET DOOR UNDER THERE, AN' INSIDE IS AN OLD TRUNK. HAUL IT OUTTA THERE AN' I'LL BE RIGHT BACK!

YOU GOT IT? GOOD!

OKAY, STEP BACK.

HAND ME YOUR KNAPSACK, BONE.

HERE.
TAKE GOOD CARE OF THIS, NOW.

BETTER COVER THIS UP WITH SOMETHIN'.

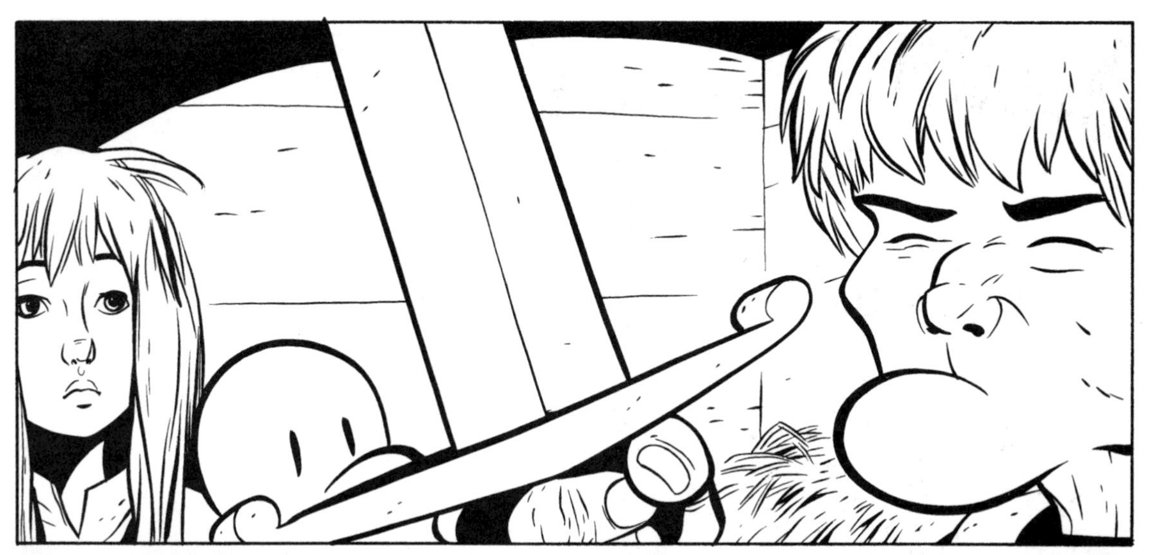

WHAT ARE YOU LOOKIN' AT? I USED TO WEAR THIS THING ALL TH' TIME!

ALL RIGHT, LOAD UP! AN' MAKE SURE YOUR PACKS ARE TIED DOWN GOOD AN' TIGHT! WE GOT A LONG WALK AHEAD OF US!

THAT'S IT? WE'RE JUST GONNA LEAVE?!
THAT'S IT.

YOU'VE BEEN AWFUL QUIET, THORN. YOU GONNA BE OKAY?
I'LL BE FINE.

NEXT: THINGS THAT GO BUMP IN THE NIGHT

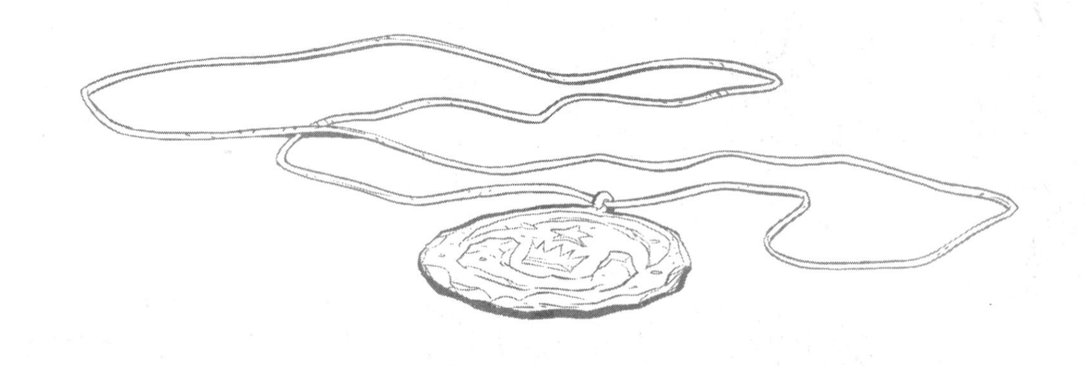

End
Of
Part One